# A Love Story

## How God Pursued Me and Found Me

## An Impossibly True Story

Samantha Ryan Chandler

*CrossBooks™*

*A Division of LifeWay*

*1663 Liberty Drive*

*Bloomington, IN 47403*

*www.crossbooks.com*

*Phone: 1-866-879-0502*

*First published by CrossBooks 2/25/2011.*

*ISBN: 978-1-6150-7758-8 (sc)*

*ISBN: 978-1-6150-7761-8 (dj)*

*Library of Congress Control Number: 2011923562*

*Library of Congress Control Number: 978-1-6150-7758-*

# Dedication

*I wrote about my life and faith for my baby girls so they would know the truth.*

# Acknowledgments

I pray that each and every person who reads this book feels the hand of God in his or her life and dares to believe the impossible.

I would like to thank my precious brother, Terry Vidrine, who in a side note gave me one sentence in my book—I hate it when you are funnier than I am!

JoEllen Bradley Jones, what can I say that tells you what my heart feels? I shall try. Your encouragement made this project imaginable.

JoEllen's precious mom, Anne, who is the mommy I always wanted. Thank you for inspiring me, and believing that I could possibly do this.

Gail Seignious, you listened to me endlessly for many years as I told you my story. When I built up the courage to tackle such daunting emotions and put them to paper, you laughed and cried while reading my first draft. I found out from you that I just might be able to convey several emotions that lived in my head and heart. Thank you.

Joseph Arnall happened to be the two hundredth person who said, "You should write a book." For some odd reason, I listened to your advice. I humbly thank you.

# Contents

# Succor

Everyone should have a Jay Wilcox in his or her life. She is my longtime friend, confidant, and my reality check on life. She has never failed to be with me through all my problems, guiding me with her perceptive wisdom.

When my life disintegrated during the obliteration called divorce, Jay was immediately at my side. In the blink of an eye, my life changed and my child was gone. I crumbled to the floor, not able to pick my head up and not able to eat. I lost twenty pounds in three weeks, and was down to only ninety pounds. Jay refused to let me stay in my condition. She would force me to eat and listened on end as I cried continually. She stood up for truth in depositions, which could have easily come at a great cost to her. I am profoundly humbled to have Jay Wilcox as my friend.

CBM has long been my sweet friend and helper. It frightens me to think of what my life would have looked like if you had not reached out to me. You were my rock and guiding force in my storm. To this day, I am amazed that you looked evil in the eye and did not back down. You stood up for truth without regard of the cost that could have been extracted from you. I love you.

Marlyn Courtney, a phenomenal piano teacher and my friend. When the courts were sorting out my rights as a mother, you continually called the guardian ad litem assigned to my case. I recall you venting your frustrations over not having the opportunity to speak of what you knew to be true. I was amazed at your tenacity and the way you finally obtained an appointment. My heart melted when you insisted on telling the courts that in the ten years of witnessing my interactions with all my babies, I was indeed an excellent mom. Thank you.

To my cherished brother, Terry, who is also my dear friend: So many times during the divorce, I would wake in fear and would not be able to fall back to sleep. I would then get into my car and drive the ten hours to our hometown. You would welcome me, and I always felt your love. I love you too, brother.

To Osanna, my sister and my friend: Your prayers and unwavering support for me will live in my heart forever. From the past to the present day, you have never failed to be there for me. Thank you, and I love you.

Kay Ramlow has been a constant friend since my early Pollyanna life. You have known me since my youthful twenties, observing and listening to all my mistakes in life. During the period of my divorce, you did not miss a day of checking in to see if I was OK and if I might need to talk about it. Even though we had a distance of five thousand miles between our homes, I felt you as my friend at my side. I love you, friend.

To my Bible study girlfriends who listened, cried, and prayed for me: I could not have conquered my overwhelming fear without your support. Thank you for holding my hand through the horror. I will never forget you.

Dr. LeDuc was my support and reminder that I was not going crazy, nor had I ever been crazy, even though all was against me. Without fail, I would leave your office with hope and words that stayed with me and kept me grounded. Thank you from my heart.

To Dr. Grace, my chiropractor and friend: I saw your concern for my health when I was so very thin. You expressed that you were worried about me. When I shared with you my dilemma concerning the courts and the guardian ad litem, you asked what you could do to help me. I remember you making endless calls to make an appointment to discuss your observations. You later shared with me how you told the guardian ad litem that my children expressed great love for their mommy and that you witnessed tenderness between us. This could have come at a cost to you with all the out-of-control actions surrounding me, but it did not deter you from stating the truth. I will never forget your kindness when I needed it the most. Thank you.

To Cary Thrift, my piano tuner: I did not have extra money, and my piano would have had to wait for its tuning, but you came anyway and tuned it for me, even though I had no ability to pay you. Your kindness touched my heart. Thank you.

To Sandy, a young and gifted woman: For several years, you would not let me pay for getting my nails manicured. This was a service I could not afford and would have otherwise skipped, but you insisted. Your kindness helped me in my darkest hour. Thank you.

# Prologue

I write my story from a place where God took my hand and led me down a path. I do not regret the horrors I have experienced, nor do I want to repeat them. I have been profoundly changed by every turn in the road that I did not choose to go down. In this book, I will speak of massive acts of unfairness and perfidy. My writings offer great insight and hope to anyone who has encountered wrongs in life that are out of control—which would truly encompass anyone who has ever taken a breath. To all who have encountered childhood abuse, I give you courage. I pray that all who read this will gain optimism for their own futures. If a skinny girl from Nowhere, Louisiana, with unnerving circumstances and totally stuck on ignorance can rise, then all can rise.

I also wish the reader to know that I did not write this book for you to read. I never dreamed it would be a book. I sat down and wrote to myself. Where were you, God, when my life was crumbling? I had a vast need to look back on my broken life and search out where was God in my time of horror. As I began my writing in small bits of time beginning from my early life, I began to see a thread, a breath of God pursuing me.

My background is life. My qualifications are that I have had more happen to me than Hollywood would ever think to write about.

If I had not lived it, I would not believe what I write about. I have been quite poor and only gazed at wealth; I have experienced poverty to the point of wondering where my next meal would come from. This has happened in more than one cycle of my life. I have also lived within the walls of the privileged, having dined with two United States presidents as well as governors in their mansions. I have dined with President Mitterrand at Versailles. I am a voracious reader and cling to self-help books. I have yet to see one written from the "privileged" world spelling out what greed is capable of doing. Having run in the circles of the very wealthy, I have witnessed the destruction of marriages where the wealthy husband does not want to share the revenues of many years of marriage.

I cofounded a not-for-profit children's ministry that is now international. I have appeared on television, and many newspapers have interviewed me. I have modeled. I have read the Bible eleven times, with fifteen years of Bible study. *Nothing* prepared me for the life I lived.

Ignorance is fixable; stupidity is terminal. I was ignorant for much of my life. My narrative contains instances of colossal betrayal, distortion of truth, vulnerability, and true love. In this book, I start by recounting the challenges of growing up and being raised by a pagan, abusive Irish mom who dallied with a spirit table. I then chronicle events showing God's hand in my life, even when I was without a clue as to who He was. It is a journey where He takes me down many paths and then prepares me for the fight of my life after marrying a man with net worth in excess of $100 million and then divorcing him.

I write of seeing an angel three times, of God's hand holding mine once, and of peering deep into Satan's eyes, which were filled with fire that was endless in capacity. My book is full of scriptures and God-given promises. God has taken me to the place where if He says it, it is done with the boldness of David. I have become David bold. I pray with his boldness, expecting no less than what is written in scripture. I have often said that if Samantha says it, then negotiation is possible, but when our Lord says He will do it, then it is not a suggestion but fact.

In this book, I tell of many places where God intervened in miraculous ways in His relentless pursuit of me. My book comes with a guarantee that the reader will laugh out loud as well as cry between a verb and a vowel, all coming from the same sentence. You then will feel happy and grateful that you were not chosen to walk in my shoes.

# Life According to Samantha

I begin to write my story with the ending unknown. All I do know is that I am a child of God, and I win. I am certain that when I am heading to a finish, God will have restored me to victory. It is His promise. It is His job.

I grew up in a very small town in the middle of Nowhere, Louisiana, to a pagan mother and a former-altar-boy-in-the-Catholic-religion father. God did not live in our home, nor was He invited in. My mother was quite abusive, and my father lived in the land of denial. My father's mom was in love with Jesus, but spoke almost no English, only French. My Irish grandparents adored me, but they were unaware of anything religious.

As a young girl, I heard ghastly stories of my mom and her antics. She had more than likely been the most beautiful woman in her Irish enclave of a village, but she had the soul of the wicked. The stories I heard were beyond frightening.

In her youth, she "worked a spirit table." This meant that several people would put their hands on the table and ask it questions. Answers came through an alphabet formed by how many times the table would rock or move. Participants even bragged about contacting a deceased spirit and gaining information that, when checked against local city records, turned out to be true. This apparently scared the group, so they took the table to the woods and left it. As the story goes, the table was back on the porch the next morning! I have no knowledge of how long this continued or what else happened, but hearing about it profoundly affected me.

I grew up in a home that felt "haunted." As a kid going out on Halloween night to trick-or-treat, I would always be more frightened of returning home than of being out in the neighborhood. This feeling never left me, even as a "mature in age and relationship" Christian. The house was unnerving. I will share more stories as I unveil my life and God's relentless pursuit of me.

I recall hearing that my birth was a medical miracle, as my mom was told after birthing my older brother that she would never conceive again.

## Heritage, Culture, Religion, Tradition:
## This Is the Product of Who You Are

It has long been a Louisiana legacy to give reverence to the dead. Every time I return home, it is tradition to go and have a beer in the cemetery. We all pile onto the tomb, chatting and drinking, often discussing memories of the deceased or even sharing details about our day. Throughout my life, I have often had picnics in cemeteries, including some in France, England, and parts unknown. Because I have done this ever since I can remember, a picnic among graves has never appeared to be unseemly to me. In fact, it seemed normal.

We have a keen responsibility to the departed. On my recent trip home, we went to the French cemetery that houses my ancestors born from 1850 onward. This is a private cemetery belonging to my dad's family. It most likely was part of their extensive land wealth, and it is not exceptional to have a cemetery be "part of your yard." We brought our Weed Eater and paint to freshen the words on the markers, in addition to the obligatory wine or other imbibing material.

Here's an extraordinary story from the long-departed Sulie Billadeau, who married the woman next to him in the cemetery, named Madame Sulie! Please take notice, Madame Sulie did not have

19

her first name engraved, just the French word for Mrs. on her tombstone. The carver called her by her husband's name and then signed his creation: "Made by MC." I have yet to see this degree of advertising in any other arena. This could seem unusual to most people, but quite ordinary to the people of Louisiana, whom we honor as well as have a laugh with our heritage.

A tidbit of story passed down from this multifaceted family. The "Sulies" had a son named Rulice Beaulldeaux, who married Prophelia. Rulice was a wealthy landowner farming several thousand acres of cotton. He had his own private train car that he used on numerous occasions to visit a New Orleans woman who was less than a lady. *En Français*, she would be called a *putania*, or in private circles, a *madam of the night*. These clandestine rendezvouses continued until all was lost—land, train car, slaves, all gone.

Back at the burial ground, I searched for Rulice's grave. He had been evicted to the far side of his parents' grave plot, only to have his wife, Prophelia, be buried next to his parents. Not only was he banished, but the spelling of the family name changed as well. His parents may have been unforgiving, but heritage and tradition has kept me grooming all their headstones well over a hundred years later. I am thinking that keeping Rulice's story alive was their best revenge.

My dad's father was colorful as well, but with decency. He spoke only French and was uneducated, yet he built several lucrative businesses. His son, my dad, was equally talented. My dad built an airplane, as one would say, "from scratch." He started this project in his garage, and when the plane outgrew its quarters, Dad had to stop and build a hangar to house the partial airplane.

On the airplane's maiden voyage, he crashed. This was only a blip on my dad's personal radar screen, as the project continued after the crash. Dad was unrelenting to fine-tune his homegrown airplane. The local paper was fascinated by such a person who would create an airplane in his garage, so the paper decided to interview dad for an upcoming local news article. The paper in Nowhere, Louisiana, did its research prior to the article. In reading the paper, I learned that Nowhere had had only one other person who had built an airplane—my grandfather! He'd built his in the late 1920s.

My relatives on the Irish side were, well, quite Irish. They loved their whiskey and their stories. My grandfather would fold his tall frame sideways into his handmade swing to have me crawl onto his lap and beg for stories. He believed (just as I do) that a good story is better than a true story. A great story that happens to be true trumps them all. I must say that this was probably not always true of the majority of his stories, but they were all good.

From my grandparents I would hear strange words that I now know came from Ireland. Food was *larapin* or *scrumptous*. *Larapin* was better than good. Sitting in that porch swing at night—and if not careful, inhaling mosquitos—and listening to bugs sing was just about the best feeling in the world.

Let me tell you a quick story from the Irish side of my family. Popa spoke of our long heritage. His great-grandmother was named Mary Ann Pharibe Ann Lorraine Zoretta Victoria Gilley. They needed to cover all the bases of whom she would be named after.

Popa never learned to drive. In his own words, he declared that there were enough fools on the highway, and he didn't want to add one more. One day he walked thirty miles to visit me in a nearby town. As I write this, I cannot fathom loving me enough to walk thirty miles just to see me. It was his love that sustained me, molded me, taught me about life and what love looks like.

Most of the time, Popa would ride a bike. If he was going to town, I would hop on the handlebars and away we would go, talking up a storm and loving being alive. I have now learned that our voyages cramped Popa's style, as he would be riding into town to have a slug of Irish whiskey that was kept with his name on it at the pool hall. After a pour was made, a mark on the bottle would keep the bartender honest.

My Popa married his wife when they were around the age of fourteen. Her nickname was Cricket, having been born the baby to a family of thirteen children where they finally decided to name her after the father! She was named Jessie with a middle name of Arizona due to the fact that the delivering nurse was from Arizona. My grandmother became a grandmother at age thirty-nine. She decided she was far too young to be called a grandmother, so we all simply called her Jessie.

Popa and Jessie saved my life, my emotional life. They were extremely poor, but they shared what they had with all, and they loved me with lack of restraint. I *knew* I was loved, and I gravitated to them. It is so ironic that the person who tormented me came from such a loving mom and dad. Life is indeed about choices we make.

I would spend my summers with my grandparents, awaking to the smell of fresh homemade bread. I don't think this miniscule woman ever slept. Her love language was giving, providing, and feeding.

It just so happened that at my grandparents' home, across the street, was a playmate. She and I would spend each day exploring their yard and the abandoned "whatevers" that populated the place. We would cut out paper dolls, walk to get an afternoon snow cone, and ride our bikes. In my summers, I would be exposed to God. My playmate would ask me to go to Sunday school with her, and each summer we had a week of church camp. Another seed of what faith looks like was being planted in my life.

# God Encounters

My first encounter with God came at age three, when I was a rough-and-tumble girl trying to keep up with my two rowdy brothers. They were jumping back and forth over a ditch that had trash and raw sewage in it. They jumped it, so I had to jump. Being a small child and quite young, I couldn't cross the gap and fell into it, only to have the artery in my right wrist severed by a broken glass bottle.

I was rushed to the hospital, but we had to wait, as there was an emergency ahead of me. The blood gushed from my small arm with the rhythm of my heartbeat. I later realized what a miracle had taken place. I had sewage from toilets in my artery at a time when almost nothing in the way of modern-day antibiotics was available. I was saved for a purpose.

Another difficult-to-explain event in my life occurred in fourth grade at the age of nine. My French grandfather was in the hospital with a relatively minor issue. I was sitting at my desk in the classroom when I instantly became unwell and raised my hand to the teacher. When she acknowledged me, instead of saying I wasn't well, I said, "I have to go home. My grandfather has just died!" She must have thought this odd, but she let me go and call home from the principal's office. I made the call and heard from the other end that my

24

grandfather had just died! How did I know? It was such an odd thing to say.

We went to the Louisiana-style wake, where I was forced to view him in the casket. I went up to it and fainted. I awoke in a back room of the funeral home, very alone and with only a low-light lamp on. My heart raced, as I was in the grip of terror at the thought of stumbling over dead bodies to find someone to take me back to my family. This is how a nine-year-old would think.

To make a long story short, I became so sick that I ran a fever for days. I didn't go to the funeral, and it was thirty years before I went to another one. I revealed earlier that my home felt haunted. During the days of the fever, I felt my grandfather in the far right corner of my bedroom, which went on for many nights. I must say that I do not believe in ghosts and hauntings, as our Lord does not leave a person to roam. What I do believe in is the power of darkness to put fear in our minds and doubt the goodness of our Savior.

# My First Visitation by an Angel

I have seen an angel three times, Satan's eyes once, and God's hand once. My first angel came to me at age six. I was on a docked boat, and my parents were away. I decided to go and look for them. I had put one leg on the dock while the other remained on the boat. The boat started to move away from the dock, and I was in the position of doing a split. All of a sudden, a woman appeared to give me her hand so I could safely take a leg away. I didn't see how she appeared or how she left.

# Saunter with God

My walk with God did not officially begin until I was age twenty-one. My childhood was a sad one, and as I have mentioned, my mom was abusive. I learned survival tactics during that time. Oddly enough, since going through that period, I have learned that according to statistics abused children have two things in common:

1. Around 90 percent grow up to be abusers. I might add at this juncture that my heart is so tender that I take ladybugs outside so they do not experience pain or death. I cannot imagine the heart it takes to inflict pain on any living creature.

2. Most abused kids feel that they deserved the abuse. I never went there. I knew my mom was sick and that if I could make it to age eighteen, her time for hurting me was up.

I cannot recall ever attending church with my mom and dad, not even the obligatory Christmas or Easter service. Yet I had a longing to go there that I cannot explain. A few times I asked to be dropped off to go to Sunday school, which always turned out to be traumatic. The kids in my class knew about God, and they knew children's songs and books of the Bible. I would leave with a sense of embarrassment and emptiness.

Then I met Helen Bass. I was in sixth grade at a new school, and she happened to be seated behind me. She was quite shy, and I have been known to chat up strangers for hours on end. It was a perfect match. I turned around and said, "Hello, you want to be my friend?"

Helen was raised in the strictest Pentecostal religion. Everything was a sin! She was not allowed to go to the movies or a school dance, to wear lipstick, to cut her hair, or to date boys. But her mom knew God. They introduced me to Him.

The first time I went to church with her, everyone was screaming and speaking words that had no meaning. I literally thought the earth would open up under my pew and I would immediately go to hell. This view of God shaped a small period of my life.

I could *never* measure up to living the way Helen lived but she acceped me as her best friend anyway. We spent every day together from our first meeting until we left high school. I made her laugh and do things she would never have dreamed of doing, and she gave me a glimpse of my need for God. In fact, this distorted view of God warped my first big decision in life. I married the boy who took my virginity, simply because I thought I would go to hell if I didn't.

I felt so unloved at home and had no guidance about right and wrong from my parents. I knew *of* God, but I did not *know* God. I had no knowledge of His love for me or His kindness and compassion for my failures without His ongoing guidance, His mercy for my sin, His righteousness, and His forgiveness. I did not know He wanted to be my friend, to guide and protect me. I thought of Him as a judge and jury, and I believed I'd better get my act together or an immediate hole would open up beneath me and slide me straight into hell: "Do Not Pass Go; Do Not Collect $200." I went on to marry three times—all failures. I will share more about this as my life with God unfolds in this book.

My first marriage was based on guilt and lasted six years. I was a mere seventeen when we married. I did graduate from high school but was not groomed for college, which would come at a much later time. I needed to make things right with God. I was very immature in life and quite naive. I did not have any basis for knowing what a marriage should look like. All I saw in my childhood home was abuse in every direction and no one showing the remotest form of respect for a human being. My first husband was clueless as well, but he did bring to the table a Godly mother. She was nurturing, and of course, I gravitated to her without restraint. I had never experienced loving-kindness on any level from a mom. She actually spent time with me! We talked, shopped, and went to movies. She even made clothing for me and taught me how to knit, cook, and give back.

She took me to church every Sunday. It was there in a small town in Louisiana that I learned of God. It was a Methodist church, so the screaming, crying, and unknown tongues were not part of the service. The people of the congregation actually had fellowship and lunches afterward! This was a new world for me.

I remember quite well the day I surrendered my life to Christ. It was in the small Methodist church that the pastor would ask people to come forward, make a public confession of their sins, and give their lives to the Lord. I am not sure I completely understood, but I can tell you that my heart would pound out of my chest each and every Sunday if I ignored this invitation. The pew would shake with each heartbeat. I was frightened to walk forward and frightened to stay in my seat. It was a physical pain that I wanted to quash.

Then one Sunday, I gathered the courage to run down the aisle. I was the only one up out of their seat in front of the congregation. The pastor asked several questions. Susequently, I was told I would have to repeat this again next Sunday! Oy, now I had to be sprinkled with water in front of everyone. I must say that the heart-pounding never occurred again, as I had made my statement of conviction with God.

# Billy, the Baptist

Now, about the sprinkling of water for baptism…I need to add that this never satisfied me. As I grew in my knowledge of the Bible, I wanted what Jesus had experienced. I wanted to be immersed, dunked—to go under and come up renewed.

Thirty-five years later, I was baptized in the River Jordan where my Savior was baptized. I had gone to the Holy Land with a Presbyterian church. However, this particular travel group left me wanting. I wanted to pray before we left for tours; I wanted to pray at night; and I wanted to study and discuss the miracle sites we had just seen. I wanted to kneel and pray at the tomb and to embrace the wall with prayer. This attitude did not endear me to the group. When I announced to the group while alongside the River Jordan that I intended to be baptized, the pastor of the group informed me that the Presbyterian religion "christened at birth." In response, I announced that if they didn't baptize me where Jesus was baptized, I would dunk myself!

Then Billy came forward, and said he was ordained in the Baptist faith and would be happy to baptize me. It was early morning on the river, with plenty of mist and rays of light coming through the trees. I was so very excited. My baby girl, age twelve, joined me. Billy's hands were shaking as he brought me under the water, and as I was lifted, my heart imagined a hallelujah chorus of angels in the background. Afterward, I always called him "Billy, the Baptist," and he would smile. I do believe in my heart that Billy was honored to be in the river of Jesus. Not long after that trip, Billy died.

# Abuse, My Mother, Wickedness, and Fear

I was around the age of four when I realized that I had a different kind of mommy. This part of the story begins with the reason why my mother acted the way she did.

My dad, my mom, and I drove to Mexico for holiday. On our return, my dad stopped at the border into the United States to file paperwork, leaving my mom and me alone in the car. This was a providential move. Also in the car was a horsefly carrying the encephalitis virus. There were two choices of who to sting. It chose my mom. I have often thought of the gift God gave me by sparing me.

A few days after our return to our hometown, my mom experienced flulike symptoms, so she and I took an afternoon nap upstairs. Afterward, she rose from the bed leaving the room stumbling, and then tumbled down the stairs. I have no knowledge of how long I sat at the top of the stairs, peering down at my unconscious mother sprawled out at the bottom. We were alone in the house, so I must have waited until someone came to check on us. I never moved from the top of the stairway until I watched the paramedics carry her away in an ambulance.

I then went to live with my French grandmother who spoke no English. She frightened me, as I could not understand her. In my confusion of what was happening in my life, I would hide under the bed for solace. I was too young to be allowed in the hospital to see my mom.

At the time my mom was taken ill, there were only a handful of survivors of encephalitis in the United States. My mom was in a coma for an extended time, and I have been told that she died several times, only to be resuscitated back to life. She was paralyzed and had suffered brain damage.

The day when she was finally able to return home, I experienced one of the most terrifying moments in my life. I sat outside atop the picnic table while she was being settled into bed. I then heard hours upon hours of screaming, sounds that one could only imagine a trapped animal would make. She had no knowledge of being married or having children, she didn't know how old she was, and she could not walk. She had to be taught everything again and to accept her husband and children as her own. She eventually was able to walk.

I have pondered whether she truly hated my dad and me or just hated having to accept something she didn't understand. The bottom line is, hate feels like hate. She loathed my dad, and she would tell him so. She didn't care much more for me either.

From the time I was four until I was able to leave home, life was dysfunctional and there was never a normal day. In that period, I did not once hear "I love you," have a conversation with my mom, or fail to fear what nightfall would bring. So very often, I had nightmares that would awaken me. I then would realize I had been screaming in my sleep. Many nights I had the same two dreams: that I was being chased and couldn't get away, and that I was falling down the stairs balled up as a tumbleweed. Just as I was about to hit the floor in my dream, my heart would jerk me awake. It doesn't take more than the IQ of a warm radish to see that my dreams were enacting how out-of-control my life was.

As my mom's brain began to heal, she would experience splitting headaches that brought on temporary amnesia. With this, great pain would follow, she then would become very sleepy and lie down. When she awoke, she would be a child again looking for her parents. Horror would come over her face as she could not figure out who we were or where she was. This was routine for many years.

She was a cruel and wicked person. I am not sure if she was this way before the brain damage, but she would use her illness as an excuse to be malicious. A few incidents, among many, stand out.

On one night of battle, I saw my mom push my dad through a glass door. I watched as both of my dad's arms and hands were cut along all sides, requiring hundreds of stitches. Another night I saw my mom hit my dad over the head with a cast-iron skillet and he crumbled to the ground. I thought he had died.

There are similar stories of what she did to me. When I was sixteen, she calmly walked up to me and took my hand in hers, only to bend back the fingers—breaking them as she looked me in the eye.

It was the eye contact that took my breath away; as I am sure I was looking evil in the face. I frequently fantasized that I was adopted, as this thought brought me great comfort. I did not want to think I had come from the womb of such a creature.

As I became an adult and God found me and my heart, I began to pray for her. I knew her destiny was hell, and this hurt me. In being vulnerable and truthful with you, I need to say that I doubted that such a person could be saved, but I prayed anyway regularly.

When my mother was in her early seventies, I heard that she had found Christ and made a public statement of faith. I went back to Louisiana soon afterward to witness it. She was amazing! She went to dinner with me, and we had a conversation! I could not believe what I saw before me. I can also state that God will withhold judgment to the last moment, hoping that people will make this choice before He sets their future. It seemed like only weeks after that weekend that mom was diagnosed with Alzheimer's. She went downhill swiftly and lost all cognitive responses for several years before she died.

# Second Visitation by an Angel

It was at my mom's two-day Louisiana wake that I saw my second angel. I told no one the thoughts I had. I was in anguish that mom's conversion might not have been a real deal, and that she was in hell. I was tormented by these thoughts, but only I knew of them.

We were at the funeral home for what seemed like endless days of a Louisiana "eat-and-greet" wake. I felt like I couldn't breathe and went outside for fresh air. I started to walk along the sidewalk away from the funeral home when a woman I had never seen before walked up to me. There were no niceties or small talk. She simply came closer and said, "I was there when your mom gave her life to the Lord," and then she walked away. How did she know who I was? How did she know the pain in my heart? She answered the question that only God and I knew was brewing inside of me. What a gift!

Several years later, my dad died. I was sitting in the same funeral home for another Louisiana "eat-and-greet" wake, thinking similar thoughts about whether my mom *really* was in heaven. After all, didn't I know fully well the extent of her wicked heart? I was sitting in the parlor with my thoughts when the pastor came over to me and said, "I was there when your mom gave her heart to Christ." I smiled and said, "Thank you."

And I have said thank you to my Savior for giving me this *lagniappe* (a French word for an extra gift, like a thirteenth item added to a dozen). We get our heavenly rewards from our earthly living, so I am not sure what my mom took with her, since her entire life was wretched, but at least she is there! She may not be in a palace—my thoughts are that she could be living atop a chicken coop—but she is there!

When I contemplate her life, only sadness comes to mind: not for me, but for my mom. I would have been a great daughter and could have been her friend as I grew older. Life is about choices we make along the way. The scripture "You reap what you sow" comes to mind. This is a spiritual law. My pastor, Charles Stanley, explains this perfectly. He says, "You reap what you sow, greater than you sow and later than you sow."

Evidence of this spiritual law is found with Saul and David. Saul was jealous of David and sought to take his life. In 1 Samuel 18:10b (NIV), it says that Saul was prophesying in his house while David was playing the harp as he usually did. Saul had a spear in his hand and he hurled it, saying to himself, "I'll pin David to the wall." But David eluded him—twice. Later, 1 Samuel 31:4 says that Saul took his own sword and fell on it. Saul reaped what he sowed. He died in the same way he attempted to kill David.

# Fear of Flying: Notre Dame

I mentioned earlier about my dad and his airplane. Well, before he built the infamous airplane that crashed, he flew manufactured planes. He would come to me in an impromptu moment and suggest we fly to Elsewhere, Louisiana, for lunch. It made me giddy at the thought of flying for lunch. I always said yes.

One return flight, we had turbulence on the landing approach. This was my first introduction to fear. I wasn't afraid of my mom or what she would and could do to me, because I viewed that behavior as normal. The idea of crashing in an airplane prior to my leaving home with unfulfilled expectations gave me pause, and fear entered in.

I kept this white-knuckle fear for many years and many, many altitude miles. It just so happened in my adult life I had opportunities to see the world. My first flight to Europe was to Paris. On the flight to France, I was horribly frightened and walked the aisles until I arrived safely.

It was a Sunday morning, and I went to view Notre Dame. My timing put me there during a service. I wanted to listen to it in French and stood by the door soaking it all in. I looked up at the cross behind the priest, thinking to myself that I was afraid to fly back. I immediately heard in my heart, "You trust me on earth but not in the air!" I would like to say this helped, but it did not.

Many years of fearful flying followed. I had managed to clock a million air miles and was still afraid. A few years prior to the annihilation called divorce (the third marriage, which I write about later in the book) from Darth Vader, God started wooing me to Him. I became immersed in the Bible and Bible study, looking for survival techniques to get me past the abusive life I was living in my third marriage to Darth Vader. It was during this process that I obtained the knowledge that God has not given us a spirit of fear. If we have fear, it comes from the other side—from Satan, Lucifer, the killer of life.

After realizing this, I became angry. How dare Satan cause me to fear flying! I am a child of God with all my rights in writing. This knowledge gave me the tools to begin fighting the fear.

As I struggled to overcome this fear, a test was presented to me. I was in a small private plane with ten other people flying back to Atlanta when the engine blew up. The pilot asked us if we saw fire, and he prepared an emergency landing. I put my head in my lap and started high-power prayer—pleading, begging God to get me safely back to my young baby girls. Going through my mind were all the things I had yet to teach them. I was keenly aware that the passengers, my friends, were talking and acting as if there was no danger. We landed at the Mobile airport and came to a stop on the runway with trucks all around us to spray if a fire should break out. I was out of that plane in a nanosecond to kiss the ground, and then I turned to the ever-so-cool people on the plane and announced that I had single-handedly prayed them safely down and that they could thank me now!

My fear of flying ratcheted to new levels. When I flew to Europe, I needed to be drugged. I didn't stop my activities, but I did take my eyes off of God in the air. I would grab a seat in first class and ask the fellow passenger next to me if he or she was afraid of flying. Almost always the individual said no, and I would declare that he or she would be by the time we landed!

This went on for a few years, and God calmly reminded me that trust is trust and I had forgotten my earlier lesson of where fear comes from. I started the process over again—sweaty palms, listening to engine noises, and then talking myself "off the roof" of fear.

God is in control. If you fear, then you are listening to Satan. I am telling you—this thought process works. When you can get your arms around your God-given rights and understand who God is and just how sovereign He is, then freedom is in sight. My belief in this principle was tested when one Europe-bound flight hit hours of dropping and sideways turbulence over the ocean. I put my sleeping blinders on, looked up, and said, "This is your job, not mine."

# My Second Baby: I Saw the Hand of God Holding Mine

Here is a bit of a backdrop on the story of the birth of my second baby. First, let me give you a bit of background data from the birth of my first baby. My first child was over nine pounds at delivery. I weighed myself that day and was 138 pounds while in labor. My point is that I am a small-boned slight-of-build person. My first baby belonged in the tummy of a woman in labor weighing in at 175! The baby was also twenty-four inches long; when you convert this to two feet long, you can then catch a visual.

My doctor was old enough to be in retirement, but sad to say, he showed up to deliver my baby. I had her naturally, but due to her enormous size I required many stitches. It took me two weeks to be up and around, and of course, my mom didn't come to see me or my baby. It was my first birth experience, so I expected them all to be like this one.

Between my first and second babies, I was learning about God and seeking Him. One week before my due date, I was in church, and I looked at the cross behind the pastor. I thought, "I am so anxious and terrified about the approaching birth." And I heard words in my heart that were unmistakably the Lord speaking to me: "Why? I will be there." I have heard the Lord speak to me only a few times, but it is always unquestionable where the words come from. They don't go through your brain; you don't think them.

As if on cue, the second baby arrived four days later, but I did not think about what I'd heard on Sunday. I went into extremely fast labor, and there was no time for medication or even getting me prepped in the delivery room. The baby was coming so fast that all the nurses were scurrying around to get ready and find a doctor—any doctor. As any mother reading this can confirm, the birthing process is quite painful.

However, I instantly went from pain to peace as I saw God's hand coming down from the ceiling to hold mine. I saw only his hand, and He grabbed ahold of mine as one would pull an individual out of water. Please note that I was not holding His hand; He was holding mine. I closed my eyes and saw and felt Him as if He and I were alone in the room. I calmly asked the nurses, "What do you want me to do?" It was an astonishing calm and peace without any pain. What I saw is now the cover of my book, God holding my hand. It is my hand photographed on the cover.

When I was due to have my third baby, I quietly said in my heart, "I wonder if I will see His hand again," and my heart heard, "You don't need it!" He was so right. And I laughed and thought about what an incredible God we serve and that He has a sense of humor as well.

# Children's Cross Connection: God's Ministry

I am a cofounder of a children's ministry formerly called Children's Cross Connection and now called Childspring International. We are dedicated to bringing extraordinarily sick or devastatingly disfigured children from around the world to the United States for donated surgeries.

I always wanted to be involved with helping children. This could have sprung from my helpless and abusive childhood, or just possibly this could have come from a wealth of love for my own children. It was a daily exercise for me to be profoundly grateful that my children were safe, not ill, or suffer from a birth defect. I often felt pained for the mothers in remote villages that had no hope for saving their child. By the grace of God, I could have been born into such a situation.

My cofounding partner and I started doing *kingdom work* with the heart that if you could change the life of one child then, it was an amazing feat. The first year we helped and saved over seventy critically and severely maimed medical kids. In my heart and actions, it was *always* God's ministry. I would pray over cases and not give up on seeking help until God took the need away.

One such case was a child from South America who had ingested lye or some type of acid that eroded his esophagus. I worked diligently for more than four years, and he was my last case to find a donated hospital and a surgeon. His surgery was a success.

I would go many months without seeing my ministry partner. We would communicate by e-mail, as time taken away from "our medical kids" was too precious to waste. She would send all kinds of cases to me, and it was typically my job to convince surgeons that they needed to operate on my medical kids for free. Then I would have to approach the hospital for a similar donation. I would have to get this arrangement in writing before my partner could apply for a medical visa from the child's country—along with donated airline tickets and a host family to take care of the child in the States. I must give American Airlines the kudos it deserves. This airline was truly amazing and a godsend; they never turned down our requests.

On occasion I would do some of my partner's tasks, and she in turn would find a doctor. My specialty involved helping the severely deformed. My passion was so great that it was hard—or some would say *impossible*—for anyone to turn me down. I was like a snake; you had to cut my head off to make me let go.

I donated my time to this ministry while my children were at school, dedicating many hours every day to these tragic children. I did not have the gift my partner had for speaking to groups, but on occasion I would speak to the press to gather more help and awareness for our cause. I would continually hone in on the fact that my three children were greatly blessed, while some mother in a hut was crying for help for her child. This thought kept me moving and motivated.

Every year, I would host a medically challenged kid. I limited their time in my home to several months, as it would take time away from finding surgeons for other kids. I would have the medical kids stay in our home as a gift to my children. Nothing is more humbling than seeing how blessed you are. My three girls learned that people sometimes look different from others, and if they had a choice, they wouldn't. These kids didn't have the luxury of choice. My girls also learned to bring a medical kid, who would be very difficult to look at, to school or to a friend's house or a game. In my opinion, it was something they *had* to learn about life.

A lesson in my ministry I had to learn, if I was to attempt kingdom work, was self-effacement. God needed to teach me. I learned it from a child whose skull had stopped growing when he was an infant. He was thirteen when we found him living in Haiti. His eyes were literally bulging out of their sockets, and he had a look on his face that said, "Help me!" The memory of his photo would wake me up at night. Unfortunately, due to the severity of his condition, my research showed that help could only be found in maybe a dozen surgeons in the United States with the expertise to break his skull and alter the shape for growth.

I kept hearing it in my heart to write to Bill Gates and ask for financial help. Trust me, I did not want to do this! But I would hear the message in my heart every day. I finally broke down and wrote a letter, which I found embarrassing to do. I received a cordial reply of denial.

I immediately heard God say to me, "Now I can use you." He needed to get me to where I did not care how I appeared; I just had to act. This attitude made me unbelievably bold after that incident. If God put it on my heart to do something, I simply did it. As a result, I saw much through the years that I cannot explain.

My first miracle was Kalina from Bulgaria. She arrived just before Christmas and, coincidently, just prior to her first birthday. Kalina had retinoblastoma, which is cancer behind the eye. She happened to have it behind both eyes. God stepped in when I asked myself, "How am I going to find a hospital just before Christmas?" What a silly girl I was! It was never about me and always about what He could do if I was obedient.

It just so happened that a friend of my husband called the house, and I answered the phone. I don't think I had ever conversed with this individual before on the phone, but this time was different. I chatted him up, only to find out that he was on the board of the largest children's hospital in the southeast. I quickly told him about Kalina. He was curious. The next day, I hand delivered information about Kalina and about our "cottage industry" of helping unfortunate kids with medical needs. Shortly after this conversation, the hospital and the surgeon agreed to donate their services and within one week, Kalina was in Atlanta for surgery.

She was operated on almost immediately. At the time of her surgery, I do believe I had all of Louisiana and half of everyone who had ever said hello to me praying for Kalina. I heard the news halfway through the surgery that one eye had been removed. I went into speed-dial to God, pleading with Him for Kalina's other eye. She kept the eye. She had the surgery and started chemotherapy.

We were chugging along five months into the chemo when I got a call that Kalina had had a setback and needed both radiation and chemo. I received the call during my Wednesday morning Bible class and asked for prayer. Today, Kalina is thirteen years old. She was baptized at age two, and I became her godmother on the same day.

Wilda from Haiti was a true success story. Sometimes when we save their lives, the children return looking the same. This was not the case with Wilda. She had a tumor in the front of her neck, and it was larger than a huge grapefruit. She was seventeen and just at our cut-off age to be considered a medical kid. Any older and you have to consider them a possible arrive-and-flee risk, meaning that they will not return to their native countries. If this happened, then his or her country would stop issuing visas for us to take any more children.

We had never had a child arrive without the surgeon and hospital in place—until Wilda. The hospital had changed its policy.

48

The surgery in another state was now no longer a "go." I found this out from the hospital while Wilda was in route by air. I picked Wilda up at the airport and took her home with me, where I tried again for a surgeon and a hospital. She was with me for over a month while I contacted every possible source.

One day I needed to take Wilda for a CAT scan, and I had to communicate to her that she couldn't move during the procedure. At this intersection of kingdom work, I had learned to follow my instincts and watch God work out the solution. I took Wilda with me to pick up one of my girls from school. My daughter asked, "Where are we going?" I calmly told her we were going to the grocery store to find an interpreter for Wilda, fully expecting to find one. I walked over to the deli and asked if anyone spoke her dialect. They said no. I then went to the bakery and asked the same question. They pointed a finger at the woman at the register. I walked over to her, and— behold—she spoke Wilda's dialect! Were we surprised? No. I had seen God move in this way too many times before in the past.

Toward the end of the month, I was at my wit's end after being turned down again and again for Wilda's surgery. She would have to return to Haiti if I couldn't find help. It was Easter weekend, so my children, Wilda, and I went to Good Friday services at my church. We walked in and took a seat. There was an enormous cross on the stage behind the pastor. At the end of the service, the pastor said that if we had anything that needed to be taken to the cross, then to come down and pray. Without thinking, I grabbed Wilda's hand,

and we flew down the aisle to be the first to arrive. I hit my knees and asked for help for Wilda.

Within one week, Wilda was in an operating room. It just so happened to be her birthday. The surgery was a huge success. Happy birthday, Wilda!

Once, I had a dialogue going with a surgeon who had performed several surgeries for our medical kids. He stopped midsentence, as if in thought, and then he asked me about my medical experience. I calmly replied, "I'm just a mom and a Christian."

# Yabsira's Story

Four-year-old Yabsira was born to a single mom in a small village in Ethiopia. She was born with severely deformed hands that were not usable, in addition to deformed legs that curled upward causing her feet to face her. Upon seeing the baby at birth, the grandmother told the new mom to kill her newborn daughter, as the child's contorted and twisted hands and legs would be a curse to the family.

The mother, afraid for her child's life, left her village and sought safety with a brother in the capital, Addis Ababa. Unfortunately, after seeing the baby, the brother also believed the child was a curse on the family and told his sister that he would run over Yabsira with a car and kill her. The only option left for the mother was to take her daughter and live with her on the streets of Addis Ababa. While Yabsira and her mother were living on the streets, our in-residence missionary discovered their plight. Yabsira came to me for surgery within weeks.

Her full name is Yabsira Bement. In Amharic, Yabsira means "gift of God" and Bement means "by faith." As I write this, it occurred to me that this precious child's name is a reality.

Permit me one more story? The head of missions at my church was KW. He had interacted with me on many occasions about the needs of my medical kids. He had seen droves of them come and go with me in church, sitting on my lap or lying in my arms. He had even escorted one child back to Ethiopia for me and had also helped to rush through a child's baptism before surgery.

During one conversation with KW, he asked me how many workers were involved in Children's Cross Connection. I gave him my partner's name and my own. He said he knew this was true for Atlanta, but he wanted to know how many there were in each state. I again answered with my name and my partner's name. He looked astonished at the realization that after seeing all the medical kids and hearing about so many others, in reality God was accomplishing much with only two people.

I say this with as much encouragement as I can muster. God used a skinny girl from Nowhere, Louisiana, to do His work. Look at several people in the Bible who were used by God. David was a murderer and adulterer. Moses stuttered yet was asked to deliver the messages from God to the pharaoh. Abraham, the father of God's chosen people, was sterile until age ninety. All that is required is to be available and obedient, and what a journey God will take you on!

I have often been asked why I do what I do, as if that could even be a valid question. Before I came into this ministry, if I read about a child in need, I would ache to help, as it truly hurt me. If it didn't hurt me, I would not have the necessary passion. Then I realized that I had been created for this purpose. God had given me a tender heart for children. When I did kingdom work, I knew without doubt that I was following God's will.

# I Saw Satan in a Dream

*Be self-controlled and alert. Your enemy the devil prowls around like a roaring lion looking for someone to devour.* —1 Peter 5:3 (NIV)

So many people want to focus only on good and ignore evil. The above scripture is truly one of the most frightening in the Bible. Evil exists. Remember Job? He was worshipping God daily when he lost everything: his children, his home, his money, and his health.

I once had a dream that, when I recall it to this day, I get chills. I was not aware of it at the time that it was a warning to me.

In my dream, I was sitting in a car with my husband (DV in later chapter titled: When Pollyanna Marries Darth Vader). DV was seated to my left in the driver's seat. On my right was another car very close to ours, not even an arm's length away. I looked to the left past my husband and saw a car explode, hugely devastating. Very slowly, as if in a slow-motion movie, I began to turn my head from the explosion on my left, first to my front view, and then my head crept to my right. I then gazed into the car parked very close to me on the right. There I saw Satan in the driver's seat. His eyes glowed with fire. I could view deeply into his eyes and see the pits of hell!

54

He said one sentence as he looked me in the eye. "[Blank] is next." He named one of my children.

At the time of the dream, this child was young and innocent, and she and I were called "Me and Mini Me." She was my shadow, my love. In reference to my dream, it seemed impossible, not plausible, to consider this as a likelihood of happening.

The dream had given me pause, but nevertheless, I did not heed its meaning. My husband and I were having extreme problems with another daughter. Our marriage was crumbling from the stress as he was and is an enabler with this particular daughter.

My husband continued to take this daughter's side, even when I would find drugs in her bedroom. He would say to her, "I believe you, not your mother." This happened almost weekly despite overwhelming evidence to the contrary. He would make excuses for her. He would reward this behavior with more money, denying the truth of my findings.

He treated her as the wife and me as the child. I will tell more of this in my chapter devoted to the destruction of my life called *divorce*.

I was given this dream approximately two years before the divorce began in full throttle. What I should have done was heed the warning and begin to pray against it. At the time of the dream, I truly thought that it was about my other child. I just couldn't see the basis of the dream happening. What I later came to realize is that the exploding car represented *my* life, not my child's. The same child named in the dream was used against me as a pawn by her father for pure greed. He took her from me, hiding her whereabouts for months.

There is much more about this in a later chapter as I am setting the stage of understanding the horror I went through leading up to *the fight of my life* called divorce. As I write this, it is *I* who need to understand and chronicle my events.

# When Hope Abandons You

*We live by faith and not by sight.* —II Corinthians 5:7

*Now faith is being sure of what we hope for and certain of what we do not see.* —Hebrews 11:1

There are a plethora of scriptures dealing with faith and how highly God esteems it. It is impossible to please God without faith.

Faith is hanging on after others have let go. Faith in God always gets results. To gain great faith, we *must* immerse ourselves in scripture, as it is a record of our rights designated by God. You cannot fight the good fight without knowledge of who you are in Christ and what He has promised. Faith and knowledge of scripture go hand in hand with prayer. My pastor says, "Little prayer, little power; much prayer, much power." When you pray, you must seek with all your heart. When I pray, I get on the floor with my face on the Bible and present myself to the Most High, humbled in His presence. Remember, it is very difficult to fall when you are on your face.

Leading up to the period of my life that can only be described as warfare, I cried out the scriptures presented below. God was preparing me for what was to come. At the time I wrote down these scriptures in the back of my Bible, I was in my fourth reading of the entire Bible. Today, I am in my eleventh reading. I promised God eleven years ago to read it each year of my life until I die.

** ** **

*But we also rejoice in our sufferings, because we know that suffering produces perseverance, perseverance character, and character, hope. And hope does not disappoint.* —Romans 5:3–5a

*He heals the brokenhearted and binds their wounds.* — Psalms 147:3

*Let us not become weary in doing good, for at the proper time we will reap a harvest, if we do not give up.* —Galatians 6:9

*Listen to my cry, for I am desperate in need.* —Psalms 142:6a

*Create in me a pure heart, Oh God; and renew a steadfast spirit within me.* —Psalms 51:10

*Be not far from me Oh God, come quickly Oh God to help me.* — Psalms 71:12

*I will refresh the weary and satisfy the faint.* —Jeremiah 31:25

*Humble yourselves therefore, under God's mighty hand that He may lift you up in due time. Cast all your anxiety on Him because He cares for you.* —I Peter 5:6

*According to your faith will it be done to you.* —Matthew 9:29

*Lord, increase my faith.* —Luke 17:5

*He gives strength to the weary and increases the power of the weak.*
—Isaiah 40:29

*I do believe, help me overcome my unbelief.* —Mark 9:24


Problems don't move God to action. Prayer moves God. Many people have problems. In II Corinthians, scripture tells us that afflictions work for us; they come to push us to another level of faith, belief, and trust. The length of time you stay in a valley is determined by the required effort on your part. You must not focus your thoughts or thinking on the things seen with your eyes, but center on what is not seen—without distractions, staying in the promises of God called scripture. We have God's strength through faith, a quiet resolve. How you react under great stress will display your character. No stress, no strength.

Fear is the polar opposite of faith. In I Timothy 1:7, in essence fear must be resisted to prevail. Satan cannot operate in absence of fear. Revelation 21 says that we are a people of God, that we fear nothing. A fearful believer is a powerless believer, and fear destroys our confidence in who we are. Needs are opportunities for miracles. We serve a God who deals with the impossible. Remember that delayed answer to prayer does not mean denial of a prayer request.

In times of great adversity, marinate in the book of Psalms. David was a man after God's own heart, and he knew how to access God's power. In Psalms, you quickly see David's boldness with God and how he handled daily disappointment. David was also my best friend in my time of crisis.

# Holy Land Trip with the Frozen Chosen

As I tell of this experience, keep in mind that I am not judging the denomination but the crowd from the church on the tour. This trip took place a few years before my life imploded with the obliteration called divorce. At the time, I was desperate to hear from God. I had taken my marriage vows in earnest: for better or for worse. I seemed to own an abundance of the "for worse." My husband was quite abusive and often cruel, which I will address in a later chapter. I argued with myself every day about whether or not I could remain married. I was so concerned about the effect divorce would have on my children.

One day I announced to the family that we were all going to the Holy Land with the church we were currently attending, including taking my sister and my husband's sister. I presumed that all would benefit from a good dose of undiluted God.

We all rode on a bus from Egypt, through Jordan, and on to Israel. I expected each morning and evening to include full-blown prayer, analyses of places parallel to the corresponding places where Jesus spoke and taught, and good Southern worship. However, I could have obtained more spiritual activity from a visit to my local McDonald's on a Saturday morning.

One such event was at the Wailing Wall in Jerusalem. My sister and I wandered away from the group. Approaching the wall, we began to pray, and as we prayed we were overcome by the immensity of where we were. We were genuinely getting into serious, gut-wrenching prayer when someone tapped me on the shoulder and said, "Hey, we are all on the bus waiting for you two. We found a burger place down the street, and we want you to hurry it up."

I spoke earlier of my baptism in the River Jordan, but what I didn't expound on was that most of the group stayed on the bus during my baptism and some were in the gift shop. They all seemed vexed at my taking valuable time from their day.

Now I will share two very special events that happened among God's chosen and the land heaven will occupy one day. I took the day off from the group and went back to the garden tomb of Jesus's burial site. A few days earlier, this place had been packed with tourists. This time I arrived alone, and not one person was in sight. I quickly went inside, thinking I would have a few seconds before being disturbed, and I knelt on the stone in front of the spot where the body of Jesus had lain. I began praying, and then my prayer turned into begging and then back to prayer. I lost myself in my conversation with our Savior. When I had wept enough and then pleaded enough, I arose and left. Caught up in the emotion, I sat just outside of the tomb in thought. I had spent at least twenty minutes on my knees without one person coming in! God had given me the time alone with Him, and as I sat on the bench and felt that I was finished, the tourists came.

The other astonishing event happened on the bus early one morning. Before we boarded the bus, I chatted with a fellow traveler, Betty. Betty was not feeling well when we left the hotel. My large group always sat in the back of the bus, even though my baby girl had been carsick for several days. The "seat constabularies" had taken over the front section of the bus and never offered to let us sit up front so she might not be as sick. On this particular morning, I asked politely if my daughter and I could sit in the first row because it might help with her nausea.

Betty was sitting in the middle of the bus. From the front, I heard, "Betty, wake up! Betty, wake up! Betty, wake up!" It was very quiet with no one speaking. My sister ran forward and grabbed my hand and said we needed to pray. I grabbed her, my daughter, and the two people behind us. I closed my eyes and prayed. All of a sudden, I felt a powerful rush, a swoosh of air that fell from the ceiling of the bus and rushed past us. It felt like a storm force going by. I quickly opened my eyes and said, "Did you feel that?" It was the Holy Spirit of God or perhaps an angel, but within a second of the whirl of wind, Betty came back to life.

On another morning, I asked my husband if we could depart from the group and go into the old section of Jerusalem. I wanted to hire a guide to show us the places that we had seen as cameo appearances on a previous visit with the group. We found a guide named Louis, but truth be known, I believe Louis found us. We strolled through the city at a leisurely pace with Louis showing us the crack in the stone under where Jesus was thought to be crucified! A church is built over the site now, but Louis knew how to go below floor level to find where the earth cracked open when Jesus took his last breath. Remember according to scripture when the sky went dark? This was the kind of tour I was salivating for!

We had lunch at a sidewalk café with Louis. Louis looked at me with tears in his eyes and stated, "You have so much pain." He spoke a bit more of this, and I wondered how he knew I was an abused child. Now I realize that he was addressing the future. After all, we were in the Holy Land where God's heart dwells. How did Louis know that what I was soon to go through was far greater than anything my mother could ever have done or thought of doing to me?

# Living on the Edge of a Precipice:

# My Marriage, or When Pollyanna Married Darth Vader

This is such a difficult time to write about. This twenty-two-year period of my life was even more painful than the abuse heaped upon me by my mother. I had spoken my marriage vows before God and said *forever*. It was a vow to my Savior, not just to my husband, and I did not take it lightly.

I dated the man I refer to as Darth Vader (DV) for more than three years prior to marriage. I rarely saw him two days in a row, so our courtship allowed his darkness to remain hidden. It was a fairy-tale wedding at a Southern plantation with many guests. My wedding present to DV was a billboard. As our guests drove to this small town in Mississippi, they read my pledge on the sign. It read: "Dear [blank], I love you so much I can't stand it," and I'd signed my name. I really did love him, but in retrospect, I didn't know him. Even after twenty-two years of marriage, I did not know this man any better than I had on our first date. Beware of secrecy.

We were married six months when I glimpsed who he was. He was profoundly wealthy and powerful but engulfed in greed and a love of money that Hollywood has yet to write about. He is the poster child for the scripture that says, "It is easier for a camel to go through the eye of a needle than for a rich man to enter the kingdom of heaven." The Eye of a Needle is a gate in the wall of the old city inside Jerusalem. In biblical times a camel had to stoop to go through the gate to enter. It is humbling to bend down. I understand this scripture. It is not that your money curses you; it is your love of it, and then it owns your soul.

In the early months of our marriage, we went to live in Europe for a year. At the time I truly did not think it too strange that I had no money for six months as we were traveling through countries with several currency exchanges. The realization of what I had gotten myself into by marrying such a guarded and mysterious man came in Portugal while living in a rented home. I asked for money to shop for groceries. Upon my return, DV quickly asked for the change back! He had only given me the equivalent of $20. I was floored. Who was he that he denied a dollar or two to his wife?

The reality became crystal clear to me as I went into the garden and sobbed. I had only $176.00 in a US bank account. This was all I had to my name. I had given up my job, and my house was for sale. He had my passport. Several days later, coming out of the fog of what to do next, I came to the conclusion that it would be prudent to find out why I felt so badly. I was *pregnant!*

He was none too happy hearing this news. In fact, according to his own sworn testimony in our divorce, he had committed adultery at the six-month point in our marriage. It was just one more shock to discover that he had sought out another woman while we were still in our honeymoon phase.

I had a decision to make: to leave and raise this child on my own or to make the best of my marriage vows. I must add at this juncture that a particular tidbit of information surfaced that persuaded me—or let's say, colored my view of what the future might hold for me.

One week prior to our wedding that was due to take place the next Saturday, DV had told me he couldn't marry me but he would live with me as his alternative. The wedding being a few days away, well, it could just be a party instead. I immediately refused and told him he was not going to take the best years of my life and that I took commitments seriously.

On the Tuesday before our Saturday nuptials, he had come to me and said he'd simply had cold feet. He would indeed marry me as planned, but I needed to sign a few papers. I went to *his* attorney to read the papers, which stated that in the event of divorce, I would get nothing! This would be the case even if I had been married to him for thirty years…I would always have nothing! I thought about it, but the "Pollyanna" in me came to the conclusion that it was only about divorce and that I had every intention of making our marriage work. How wrong and how dumb can one skinny girl be?

I soon found out after the wedding that the agreement was about how we lived as well as what would happen if I left or if he should tire of me and wanted me out.

Twenty years into our marriage it became apparent to DV, as he was planning my demise called divorce, that this prenuptial agreement was invalid for three reasons. It was signed under duress and given to me just days prior to our wedding, it was handled by DV's attorney, and it was grossly unfair without his financial statement attached. To this day, it surprises me that it took him so long to figure this out!

After just a couple of years of marriage I knew that the document was illegitimate, but I kept this knowledge to myself as I wanted DV to desire to share with me, not forced. It had never been about the money and always about wanting DV to merge his life with mine.

We muddled through Europe for several months after the first money encounter, but the veil was off the blossom. I was now starting to outgrow my clothes as the pregnancy moved along. I refused to take any money from him, even to buy maternity clothes. This did not even appear on DV's radar screen that we had problems, as he was quite happy to count his coins every night and tell himself what a handsome man he was.

We returned to the States during my seventh month of pregnancy. I had not touched money for several months, and for *appearance* sake only, DV was disturbed. Thus began endless therapy sessions that plagued our marriage. He could always find a therapist who agreed with him. I find it fascinating how money and not much of education makes a "good therapist."

DV would hand me a check and say, don't ask me for *anything* for one year. I'd had more disposable income when I was poor than I did from the amount he offered. I would rip up the check and hand it back to him, telling him that the giving needed to come from his heart. I wanted him to *want* to give, to care about my needs, and not to act out of fictitious guilt.

At such a time as this, enters the therapist. He or she and DV would beg and plead for me to "be reasonable." They just didn't get it. In trying to bridge this chasm, one therapist suggested that Darth Vader and Pollyanna write out what we thought was a sensible way to live. The wisdom of the day required DV and I to come at different times to discuss what each of us had written.

There I was, sitting in a therapist's office, nine months pregnant, struggling to learn how I was expected to live. The therapist outlined what DV had said were acceptable expenditures for his wife. He also stated what he considered unacceptable. I looked at the list of what DV would pay for and what he would *not* pay for. I found out he did not even want to buy my magazines! I should have been grateful that food was on my list of acceptable expenses. I fought back the tears and slowly rose, leaving the office shaken to my core. It was a defining moment. I now clearly understood what life was to look like when one has no choices. I was living in a world I did not have.

My first physical abuse by DV was approximately at the two-year mark of our marriage. We had left the baby with a sitter and were off for a Saturday something. I hadn't eaten, and the morning was wearing on, so I suggested a quick ice cream cone to tide me over until lunch. I asked DV if he would like one, which he declined. What the reader could not know by my writing is that I am thin and need nourishment on a regular basis. I did not get out of the car to buy half an ice cream cone but a whole one.

I began to nosh the ice cream at the speed of light. DV bends over my ice cream and tries to take it from me. I told him I was hungry and would be happy to go and purchase one for him. His anger became rage as he screamed that I was incapable of sharing. He hit the ice cream out of my hand so hard that he broke my finger. The hand surgeon showed me from the x-ray that a piece of bone was chipped off. Can you imagine how hard you have to hit someone to achieve this result?

The years chugged along. In my misery, I began to lose myself. I was no longer playful, and happiness had moved off my face. My husband's cruelty hit new heights with each passing year. I immersed myself in my children and my medical kids from the ministry I had cofounded.

Years into my marriage, my precious dad had cancer. He fought the good fight, and lay in a hospital bed in a coma state. At that time, we lived several states away from Nowhere, Louisiana. I got the call that the end was near. DV dropped me off at the airport to go alone and watch my dad die. In retrospect, I should have been exceedingly appreciative that I didn't have to take a taxi.

My two brothers and sister were in the hospital at Daddy's bedside, with their spouses by their sides. We were like this for a cloud of days, afraid even to go to the restroom for fear he would die while we were away. As my daddy grasped at life, each had someone to hug. I had no one. I had married Darth Vader, and his concerns were far greater than mine. He was important to the community, with no time for grief or compassion for such a person as a mere wife.

Out of decency and because my friends called DV to check on me, he believed, for *appearances* sake that it would be prudent to call me each day. I was so hurt that he was not with me and I became vocal. On the morning of my dad's death, DV and his entourage graced the hallways of the hospital. I was in the room sitting on the hospital bed holding my dad's hand, reassuring him that he was not alone. I watched my dad's monitors go silent and waited endless minutes before the nurse said, "He is gone."

Stunned by what I had just witnessed, in addition to not having slept for days and not remembering the last meal I might

71

have eaten, I left dad's room. DV and I walked to the hospital garage to travel to my hometown and gather with my brothers and sister. My dad was not even cold before DV looked at me and said, "You are the most selfish person I have ever known!" This statement was in response to my wanting him with me while I watched my dad die. It has gone down into the archives of my life as one of the cruelest moments I've ever experienced.

DV had a whole handbag of viciousness and malice. He would often call me a thief. He would micromanage the household credit cards, coding each charge. If an item looked like it could possibly be for me, he would accuse me of stealing from him. You must understand that the check given to me on January 1 of each year was to tide me over until the next year and cover all my needs. Remember, DV is not a generous person caring about anything or anyone but himself. His philosophy is if three is good, then one will do, always giving less than needed.

Once, while on a trip with DV, I saw a piece of costume jewelry and was naive enough to suggest that I wanted it. His reply was, "You have your money." This experience of raw pain taught me never to ask for anything. After our divorce, I learned that he was worth multimillions of dollars. Greed and a black heart were his identity.

I have mentioned the swinging doorway of therapists in our life. This was ongoing and uneventful. DV could buy truth. They always agreed with him. He could leave the sessions with his ego intact, feeling like the most amazing man alive and totally convinced that he was a good person. We were taught fluent therapist-speak. DV loved to battle, and during one mindless conflict, I announced that what he was doing was hurting me. His retort was, "You deserve to be hurt!" I publicized this as foreplay to the divorce, so people might understand his depravity.

I learned during the separation and divorce that DV had planned my demise for five years, moving assets, trusts, and so on. He was also increasingly abusive.

A few months prior to our inevitable departure from the facade of marriage, one of my children was deeply involved in drugs. I was fearful that she would have another car accident, as she had had five between the ages of fifteen and eighteen, with two cars no longer usable or worth repairing as the damage was so great. I had found a photo in her room that showed her driving with her foot on the steering wheel, and through examination by a magnifying glass, I saw that her speed was a hundred miles per hour. Upon showing this to DV, his retort was that *I* drive fast! His hatred of me was so great, and his denial of the problem floored me. He treated me like the child and the child like a wife.

I was given no respect and no say in the outcome of our children. I had been rendered helpless. Upon realizing that my child was in danger, I grasped for help but to no avail. My blood pressure was skyrocketing from extremely low to my heart pounding in my chest, producing migraine headaches. I thought it wise to have a complete physical with a stress test performed by a cardiologist friend. He knew my issues at home. He came into his office with the results and stated that he had good news and bad news. The good news was that I had the heart of an athlete; the bad news was that my life in shambles was causing the high blood pressure.

I found out that during this same period of time (and even going back a year) DV had been writing about my "behavior" in a journal. When I found his writings, I saw what he had written, *She grabs her chest in church and breathes heavily.* It read like a stalker watching my every move. I will expound on this more when I describe the period after the divorce was filed, and why he was chronicling my every move.

In retrospect, I now know that DV needed to ratchet up his plan to overthrow our marriage and me, as he was about to sell a multimillion-dollar company. At the time we were living together still married, I had no knowledge of his ownership or the existence of the company. I found out about it a week after our sudden separation on a long sleepless night when I Googled DV's name and the business appeared. Within a week or so, DV completely disappeared from the internet in all fashion and shape. I am sure this was no easy feat and quite costly too, but compared to giving his wife of twenty-two years half his money…well, do the math, a no-brainer. It's a tribute to the terminally greedy. In addition DV had already found out his marriage contract was worthless. A new route for my disposal without money must be formed, and quickly.

I mentioned earlier that DV methodically planned my overthrow for at least five years. Well, prior to our separation, he "found God." He went to a Wednesday morning Bible class and scheduled prayer time. A year before his premeditated plan for my departure, DV started broadcasting to his "support group" that his wife was ill and asked that they pray for me. By "ill," he meant *mentally* ill. This information came to me via a woman who had seen the e-mail. All this was setting the stage for my demise.

The summer before his game plan was implemented, I took my baby girl to our mountain home and announced to DV that he had the summer to figure out if I could be put into the top ten of things he liked. His abuse was horrendous, and I would awaken every day saying, "I can do this; I can do this. I just have to make it until my last baby graduates so the children will not be unsettled." I had no idea that he'd had a divorce attorney for several months prior to my announcement.

From that point on, it became a God thing in how I discovered things and stumbled onto DV's secrets. His assistant went to my best friend, deeply disturbed at something DV said to her in a moment of rage. He yelled in a fit of anger, "I could have her committed for this." I was stunned to hear these words, as the idea of having someone committed doesn't just come to mind in a fit of anger.

I took her warning to heart and started going through the file cabinets at home, as his assistant worked from our house. I started finding documents that said I didn't have any share in our homes and all of what I thought was our community property was in DV's sister's and father's names or a trust that DV totally controlled. I went into silent panic, not sure what was happening but keenly aware that I needed to be quiet and smart until I could get a grip on things.

DV's assistant was concerned as well, as she attempted to fill in the blanks on a bucket-load of secrecy. She told me of a safe that DV used, and I told her there was no safe in our home. She assured me that he went to one in our home regularly. I had been the designer of our quite large and prominent home. I took out the plans and studied them, noticing that the mechanical area on the plans had been moved and was not as drawn. I had been unaware of this change.

I got a ladder and began looking for something but was not even sure what to look for. I was trying to find the change made in the plans and why it was changed. The mechanical in the house plans would have been near or behind the wine cellar. I spent days going through this area to find that in the wine cellar there was a lock just behind a space, where a bottle would hide it from view. I used my ladder to look above the two walls that joined and saw a plate over hinges. I got a screwdriver and took off the plate, and saw that this could operate as a swinging door. I waited until DV was out of town and called a locksmith, telling him that I'd lost my key. He arrived and got the lock to open. To my astonishment, the two sides swung open to reveal a secret room!

In this room were four machine guns that turned out to be an Uzi, an AK-47, and I cannot remember the brands of the other two. I also saw piles of ammunition, twenty-seven bags of silver, tubs of documents, and a safe in the concrete floor. The locksmith saw the machine guns and later called the FBI.

I was away from home when the FBI showed up, and my oldest daughter opened the door to find two men with badges. They did not have a search warrant at that time, so she didn't let them in, but she immediately called me on my cell phone in disbelief. I am not sure what I told her, but I tried to be casual. I then called an attorney who contacted the FBI, and somehow they dropped the pursuit.

I was so afraid of DV and was not sure what was happening in my life, so I took the cautious route. With all my heart, I now wish I had not stopped them from meeting DV at the airport with a search warrant. My outcome would have been entirely different if this had taken place, but I had to go through what I did to learn what I have learned. We cannot short-circuit the "I am going to take you to another level" in the faith process.

I took the tubs of documents, headed to my local copy center, and made duplicates. My thinking was that whatever was in it was meant to be secret and that I needed to know what it involved. I returned the tubs to the safe before DV returned home, and nothing looked out of sorts—except my life.

Two weeks later, DV was out of town again, and I capitalized on this time to find out what was in the safe in the floor. I went into the secret room and stared at the safe. It had the name of the manufacturing company, complete with the town where it was made: Ventura, California. It also had the name of the local people who had installed it. I called the local installers, acting like a ditzy blonde. (Sorry blondes, but brunettes need all the help they can get.) I stated that I had lost my combination and gave them the model number. They announced that they would have to call California for the combination.

I got the combination, but it didn't work. I sat and stared at the safe, looking for an answer as to why it didn't work, only to see the words Ventura, California, again. I took a chance and called them, asking for customer service. I told them my issue, and they told me they couldn't help me over the phone. I continued to chat with her and gave her my combination. She blurted out that I had the numbers in the wrong order. Whew! I went into the secret room, only to find that I still could not open the safe. My time was running out before DV's return.

I called another locksmith, telling him that my combination didn't work. Thank God for hands and ears such as this locksmith had. He could feel with his fingertips that with time, the lock had changed a digit or so. He opened the safe, and I then rushed him out of the house. In the safe were mounds of gold Krugerrands and enough documentation to scare me for my future. I saw a typed ongoing analysis of my day-to-day activities, written in the style of…words fail me, but stay tuned as this unfolds.

For some unknown reason that I cannot fathom, I took the gold and left the silver. I put the gold in the trunk of my car with the intention of confronting DV about all that I had seen. Now, remember that at this juncture I did not know that DV had had a divorce attorney for several months and was biding his time to make his plan work. What he did not count on was that being a child of God, I had help from on high.

The next morning after breaking into my own home, I took the documents to an attorney friend and tried to glean what was going on, knowing that life as I knew it would never be the same again. I even forgot that I had a trunk-load of gold in my car. I told her the story, and she became quite concerned. I signed a few papers, giving her permission to do whatever attorneys do, and returned home with the full intent of confronting DV and asking many questions.

I entered my kitchen to see DV and a man named T. J. Ward. I introduced myself to this stranger, and he flipped a badge on me! I was convinced that he was going to arrest me. I felt faint. He started to ask me about the gold, and I said I wanted to speak with my attorney of now thirty minutes. I had heard this request in a movie, and for some reason it came to mind. I refused to answer the badgering questions that treated me as a thief in my own home. I asked T. J. Ward to leave, again and again, as he was in my home. He ignored me. I wanted to leave but realized that my car keys were missing from where I had left them and my garage door was locked. My head was spinning; I ran upstairs to my bedroom and tried to contact an old friend I truly trusted. My situation was quickly becoming a "who's who" of people I could trust.

I stayed in my bedroom for an hour or so, only to find DV and T. J. Ward on the balcony outside of my room, pounding on the windows. DV was shouting for all to hear, "Don't hurt yourself!" I was thinking, *I am the last person whom I currently want to hurt!* Remember this statement from DV, as it will fall into place with his upcoming plans. I called my attorney from my bedroom, telling her to file a separation, as I could *never* stay married to someone who could have me arrested!

It was now getting to be time for me to pick up my baby girl (to protect their names, I refer to my three daughters as First Baby, Middle Baby, and Baby) from school, but I didn't have transportation. My friend called another friend, who drove over to get me so I could go to my baby girl. We left in her car. I obtained my child and asked my friend to give me some time alone with her. We walked over to a quiet bench at school, and I took my ninth-grader onto my lap, wanting to protect her from what I now knew and from so much of what I didn't know. I told her that Mommy and Daddy were going to separate and that we needed time to work on our marriage. I told her that she should spend the weekend with my friend, as she had a daughter the same age. I remember what I told her as if it were minutes ago and prophetic. I told her that there would be much she would not understand. I told her to use God in her heart to decide what a lie was and what she knew to be true. This had to be from God's mouth to her ears, as I am truly not that smart.

Have you heard that timing is everything? It certainly is true. Upon my return from picking my baby up from school, DV was being served divorce papers and that I had filed for divorce with the reason being abuse. Let it be known that if you do something in life, then you must be prepared to live with the outcome of your actions.

As timing would have it, my oldest baby was moving to another state to start her master's program in education. I had planned to drive with her and set up her apartment, buying what she needed and generally doing mommy duty. My friend of many years begged me not to go, but I could only answer that my child needed me. She had an accurate hunch that I should not leave.

I started the twelve-hour drive with my daughter only forty-eight hours after DV had been served the divorce papers. I set up my daughter's apartment and purchased all she needed in two days. I flew back home in order to leave the next day with my middle child going off to college, who needed the same assistance from me in setting up on the opposite coast from where we live. I flew for five hours and rented a car to go and look for apartments for my second daughter. I was keenly aware that I needed to get back to my youngest baby who was still with my friend. I returned home on Labor Day weekend.

DV had picked up my youngest from my friend's house without telling me of this change. I had rushed back to be with her, knowing she needed her mommy. He had started his scheme. On Friday at 5:00 p.m. on Labor Day weekend, my attorney received a notice for an emergency hearing scheduled on Tuesday morning following Labor Day. The hearing was to verify my sanity! There was no time to get witnesses or testimony or facts.

My child at this time was fifteen years old and not a baby; and I had an unblemished life. Remember I had started a children's ministry to help children from around the world. I was a Girl Scout leader, a Sunday school teacher, and a mom totally involved with her children. This was done out of greed on DV's part, as he had tried to put our daughter in a boarding school immediately after the hearing. He did not want to raise her. What motivated him was the fact that he was a wealthy man and child support is based on a percentage of income. If I had been given the opportunity, I would have taken her without money. All I wanted was my child. I had never been without her.

My oldest daughter flew right back home to testify at the hearing, and on Labor Day she gave an affidavit to my attorney, stating that I was an excellent mom and that if her dad was granted custody, he might allow her sister to do drugs just as he had enabled the other. The judge had this statement as well as my daughter waiting in the back to testify on my behalf.

What I did not know until I arrived in the courtroom was that DV had gone to my daughter's two therapists, who had the knowledge and education of a social worker, and had them write affidavits that DV's attorney drafted giving testimony against me. This affidavit took my daughter away from me in ten minutes. Judge Shoob never asked to speak to my oldest daughter. She had granted the emergency hearing based on two therapists—one who said I was self-centered and the other one who said I could hurt my child. This same "joke" of a therapist received $10,000 from DV. I just cannot fathom ruining someone's life for *only* $10,000. I would think they would have at least demanded more for my life.

Judge Shoob should have thought this one through. If the two "jokes" were indeed my therapists', then the courts would have had to order them to volunteer my medical records, as this is privileged information. If they were *not* my therapists, then they had no knowledge of my conduct. It just so happened that D. O'Neal and K. Clark were the therapists for my daughter with the drug problem. I had seen O'Neal two times, begging her to see what the father was doing. I had seen Clark maybe five times, and this was after my daughter was caught with possession of drugs in our home as well as in her car. I explained that her father prevented me from helping my child and did everything in his power to enable the behavior.

I left the courtroom stunned and in disbelief of what I had just witnessed. Justice was not served, and my rights as a loving mom had gone unnoticed. During the ten-minute period the judge used to make the decision, DV took out his Bible and started reading it: so very pious, so very theatrical. It so reminded me of the Pharisees and the Sadducees of the Old Testament, in the temple, wailing for all to see and admire.

I went numb and almost crumbled, but I had to maintain strength as two of my children were nearby. This was where it became so odd. The child who had been taken from me moments before wanted to go to dinner with her sister and me! I firmly believe that in her immaturity, she had not understood the ramifications of what had just taken place. We went to dinner, and her dad picked her up promptly from the marital home at a specified time. Just prior to DV approaching the driveway, she and I lay under the stars talking, with me trying to give her understanding of what had just taken place. What do you say when everything in your life is mimicking bizarre?

The next day, my daughter called me and said she wanted to come home. She asked me to pick her up after basketball practice. My heart stopped, and I held my breath. I arrived at school early, just needing to gather my thoughts. She got into my car, and the first thing I said to her was that I would never take her dad away from her, trying to reassure her that life could possibly be normal. I stated that he was invited to our Thanksgiving and Christmas extravaganzas.

That was a Wednesday evening. On Friday, I planned to take her to the football game at her school, but as bad decisions would have it, I had a migraine headache and did something uncharacteristic of me—I dropped her off alone and saw to it that she sat with friends and their moms.

As I look back on the chain of events, it just had to happen this way. Satan was no doubt in control of all that made no sense, but God had a larger plan that has taken many years for me to see. I stayed home on that Friday night, which gave an old friend from New Orleans on DV's payroll a chance to help him in his plan. She was my friend of thirty years. I later found out that she had been his lover during our marriage.

What do you think trumps in life? If you guessed money, sex, and lies, you win the right to vote on who in my life was more justified in selling me out. When you vote, you will have my brother (who professed to despise DV), my friend of thirty years, and my associate pastor who counseled us and also received enough money from DV to start his own church but never acknowledged my pain or the two therapist-jokes. Please wait, as all will be revealed prior to your vote.

On Saturday morning, the friend of thirty years insisted that I go to breakfast. I left the house, not knowing that she had told my baby that I had broken into her computer the night before and that was why I hadn't gone to the game. I returned from breakfast to find my child gone, as DV had picked her up. A note on the kitchen counter said that she could not live that way. I quite understood her confusion, as life was not supposed to be that way, and a father would always tell his daughter the truth, right?

I kept thinking that she would return, as we had never been without each other. Days rolled over into more days, and then I took the opportunity to go to her basketball game. She was on the floor with her teammates, and DV was standing in the hallway between us. She continued to look from him to me. When halftime came and she ignored my presence, I got up to leave, fighting tears. DV advanced on me like a linebacker in a football game. I have never been quite so stunned and mortified, but then again I still had more to come that would stretch this statement. He was trying to prevent me from going to my child or speaking with her! I left. Little did I know that it would be over four months before I would see her again. Every day I sent e-mails to my attorney, begging for the right to see my child. I was ignored on all levels.

DV had gone to our daughter's school, demanding that they bar me from setting foot on campus. I heard this directly from the assistant, who was in disbelief at hearing it. The headmaster denied DV's request, asserting that he knew my character, as I had volunteered many times at school. This was a Christian school that could not be bought.

So DV took her out of this school and moved her to another one that I was not aware of. He knew if I had any contact with "Mini Me," she would return to me. After all, he needed the time to brainwash her into believing that the reason she could not see me was that "her mom was crazy." For several years, my child believed I *was* crazy.

Nine months after the school drama, I believed that I would have my day in court and clear my name. I had the two "jokes" called therapists subpoenaed for underoath depositions. This was scheduled for a Friday. The Thursday night prior to my garnering the truth, DV convinced my daughter to sign papers late at night that stated that I had no rights and that she picked him to be her sole caretaker!

DV was afraid that people would find out who he truly was. He envisioned that all thought him a pay grade below angelic. He carried his Bible throughout life, pontificating sage promises and going soft in his voice, his eyes full of meaning, announcing that he "will pray for you." Run fast from such a person. Words are meaningless. Actions reflect the heart.

This creature put his money ahead of all that was precious to me: my children. They all have been damaged to some degree from his tar-filled heart and mind of greed. Not once did he, in the years of fighting me for divorce and stopping at nothing to see me homeless (with his first choice being seeing me naked on the streets), ever back off of Plan Greed. It took two years of endless debt on my part and fighting with him to dissolve a twenty-three-year marriage. After my child was removed from me, I lost all will. My friends and my oldest child were so very concerned, as I had dropped twenty pounds in two months, weighing ninety-seven pounds at five feet six inches.

How do you fight evil? How do you fight a powerful man with no conscience? How do you ever win? The short answer is—on your knees. I have come light-years ahead in faith to where I could never have gone if my life had not read like a bad soap opera. My answer to most problems is simple. I was married to DV for twenty-something years—I can do *anything!* You truly do not know your strength until you are asked to pick up something.

DV had a battle plan that any four-star general would have coveted. He planned it for years and it was finely executed. He could write the book on how to throw away your marriage, damage your children, and have the most gold in the end.

After my child signed away my rights, DV became superior about my having no contact and prevented every opportunity for me to see her. He had moved her to a school that was a half-hour drive each way. He, of course, did not make this sacrifice, but instead hired someone to drive her. I begged to drive her, which would have meant a one-and-a-half-hour round trip for me, just to be with her. He told me that if I showed up, he would have me arrested.

I remember so many useless fights calculated to destroy me. There were times when I would leave the courtroom and within minutes to be served in the parking lot for another contempt hearing. He did not want to solve the issue; he wanted to extinguish me. There was a time when I was accused of "stealing a painting" from one of "our" homes. My oldest daughter went to one of the four houses he owned and photographed the painting. She was clever enough to think of putting a newspaper with the date next to the painting showing it was still on the wall. This was to verify our truth in presenting evidence. How pitiful that my child had begun to think that way.

While I was living in the marital home during our separation, there was a break-in. I was away for several hours only to return to find a large door hidden from the street that had broken glass everywhere. I learned that, prior to our separation and during the time that DV was planning my overthrow, the alarm system was changed. A back window and door were no longer on the alarm. This started a real fear inside of me. DV knew he could just walk into the home even if the alarm was activated. I tried to change the alarm-monitoring vendors, but was told I would have to wait four weeks for an opening in their schedule. I was terrified, as the house sits way back from the road, and it's dark.

Everyone in the family had a key to the gate; if it didn't open electronically, they could open it manually. I had managed to get the entrance code to the gate changed very quickly, but that did not change my safety issues, as DV still had access to the house, knowing the alarm would not be set off in the bypassed area. I was also being followed by a car that stayed parked across from the driveway. I had by now learned to sleep with my bedroom door locked and still do the same to this day.

In this interim period of waiting to have the alarm changed and all windows and doors secured, I started hemorrhaging greatly and needed surgery. The surgery needed to be done as quickly as possible, but I stalled a few days, as DV was trying to get me back in court with almost no notice for my attorney to prepare. By stalling, I gave my attorney time to get through the endless demands and threats by DV.

I spoke with my doctor and shared my story. He had known there had to be a story just by looking at my appearance. I was now smaller than any clothing size for a woman, and I could now wear children's clothing. My eyes looked hollowed from lack of sleep and worry for my children. One look at me, and a person would know my life was not right.

The doctor agreed to perform the surgery the next week on the day I was to appear in court buying my attorney time to prepare. He wrote a letter telling the court of my pending surgery, and I was excused for a month to heal. The courts and DV knew I would be in surgery at a certain time on a certain day.

On the day of surgery, my friend was to take me to the hospital, as I was to be put to sleep and couldn't drive afterward. As usual, she was late to pick me up. God bless her! Being late to go under the knife and quite sick, I started to pace at the top of my driveway. I noticed a panel truck parked at the corner across the street. I also noticed a moving van parked in front of it. My friend showed up and I jumped into the car, asking her to drive near the panel truck to see what this was about. It was a locksmith! I immediately thought, *DV is going to break into the house while I am on the operating table!* I told my friend to go back to the house and that I would drive myself. I needed her to protect my home. I was certain DV would empty the home, collecting my files, and then blaming me for hiding or stealing the antiques.

Before I left, I closed the gates and poured epoxy glue into the keyhole. This is the key hole that allowed the gate to be opened from the outside on the street side. My friend agreed with me and watched the gate on a television that was in the pantry of the house. Remember that I had lived in a prominent home with all the bells and whistles of prosperity. After I drove away, she watched the locksmith drive up to the gate and reach the area where a key would go, only to see his expression of impossibility. He then picked up his cell phone, made a call, and left. The moving van left too. You may use your imagination to decide what could possibly have been happening at the hands of someone with no soul or a conscience. I don't know why the van was there, but with DV's track record it's not hard to figure out.

91

As it turned out, DV had needed to get into the attic where he had carelessly left documents that could possibly allow his wife to have some money in the divorce! How sloppy could one tiny scheming man be?

Since he had the time to preplan my overthrow, DV had cleverly managed a ten-minute meeting with each of the great attorneys in town. For the ones reading this who haven't experienced "money divorcing without paying," all the greedy-without-a-conscience men do this, as now the attorney cannot represent the wife. It has become quite fashionable, and I have heard of it many times since. I hope you have been glued to my every word and remember several pages back that DV kept me without money. This was to make sure that I could not hire a good attorney.

Our two-year battle continued as planned, and we were finally divorced. At that point, I was war-weary and truly afraid of him. One would think that DV would leave me alone at that point. Could I have possibly been so fortunate? He had my baby girl, all of our homes and furniture, and had managed not to pay alimony. I received a fraction of the value of our estate. This went against DV's plan to have me naked on the streets, so he continued to pursue me with frivolous claims and endless court battles, and chipped away at the money he owed me.

At the end of another contempt of court hearing, he accused me of stealing his furniture from the marital home, which I was allowed to live in until it was sold. This was done to get the judge to refute my divorce decree and declare me unfit to use the home. My oldest daughter was in the courtroom and watched the slander of her mom by her dad's attorney. Everyone knew that no one did anything unless it was directed by DV. I left stunned and headed to the airport. I had a flight to London where I had escaped to a few months before. In my heart, I knew DV was capable of *anything*, and I no longer felt safe. It was during this scenario that I saw my third angel.

# Third Visitation by an Angel

I arrived at the airport with just enough time to catch my flight after being in court all day. I got on the plane so very traumatized and trampled that I could not even talk to God. I spoke to no one and possessed no thoughts. I was vacant.

I arrived in London and started my endless walking, without feeling anything. I then caught a bus and stood in the middle of the aisle, which is not where I typically stand. After the bus had stopped for approximately twenty minutes, I looked around and noticed that there were only two people on this bus—myself and another.

Upon reflection, this was impossible, as we were on one of the busiest streets in London. The other woman tried to have a conversation with me, but it was impossible, as no one was home in my brain and emotions had vanquished. I could hardly look at her, but I did notice that she had a broken front tooth. How odd of me to only noticed her tooth and that I was unable to chat with her. The bus was not moving, so I asked the driver to open the door and let me out, and I resumed my endless walking.

The next day after church, I walked to another part of London that was many miles from where I'd been the day before. I looked up from my walk and—out of a London population in excess of ten million—I saw the same woman walking over to me!

She came very close to me and stopped. She said, "God loves you very much." I then did the cocker-spaniel thing, tipping my head to the side in disbelief. She spoke again and said, "I am an angel. God loves you very much." After my cocker-spaniel gesture to the other side, she said, "Yes, broken tooth and all." God knew that the tooth was all I would remember about this woman and had sent me verification.

I would like to tell you that life became good for me after that, but it didn't. I would go for several years with one daughter not speaking to me and the youngest one that DV had taken ignoring me—I am certain, out of confusion and because she was shutting down emotionally. It took six years for me to have all of my children back in my life at the same time. Words fail me to express all that I learned during this period of horror. I no longer care about anything material and have almost no desires. I went through a long period of survival and years of processing what had happened.

Today, I am healed. I pray for DV…I can't say daily, but often. He is a very sad creature and has lived in denial of his actions, believing himself to be righteous. Everything I write has been documented in court proceedings and depositions, as well as through an abundance of eyewitnesses.

My life has been changed forever. Pollyanna is dead and a phoenix has risen. I have more faith in the goodness of God than I could have ever had without going through all the turmoil that is called my past.

# Jacob Wrestles with God

*Then Jacob was left alone, and a man wrestled with him until daybreak. Then he said, "Let me go, for the dawn is breaking." But he said, "I will not let you go unless you bless me." —Genesis 32:24, 26.*

In writing this, it occurs to me that we wrestle with life, and it is said that it is always darkest before dawn. Jacob's blessing came before dawn. Could it be that just when the battle is at its worst our breakthrough of blessing is close at hand?

In Jeremiah 29:11 (King James Bible), the scripture says, "'I know the plans that I have for you,' declares the Lord, 'plans for welfare and not for calamity; to give you a future and a hope.'" And in Luke 11:10 (NIV) it says: "For everyone who asks, receives; and he who seeks, finds; and to him who knocks, it will be opened. "Now suppose one of you fathers is asked by his son for a fish; he will not give him a snake instead of a fish, will he? Or if he is asked for an egg, he will not give him a scorpion, will he? If you then, being evil, know how to give good gifts to your children, how much more will your heavenly Father give the Holy Spirit to those who ask Him?" (Luke 11:9–11).

# Jack, My Love: My Earthly Life

*Within your heart, my love has found a home.*

Loving Jack was the sweetest thing I have ever done. If God had come to me and asked me what I wanted in a husband, Jack would be more than I would have thought to ask for. He is an amazing guy, and he makes me believe there are still amazing men. Before Jack, I was suffocating in an emotional vacuum.

Jack was a chance meeting after many years of running away from a magnitude of pain. At the time we met, I was far from being able to want, feel, or commit to anyone. It had been many years since the annihilation called divorce and I was a self-described "serial dater." I would awaken each day with no purpose, trying to wear myself out with extreme exercise, parties, and travel. I could not have been more shallow than I was at this time in my life. I would have several different dates each week, and when it came down to the kissing stage, I would bow out and start over with another group. I would tell myself, "The man I marry has not been born yet." I even told myself that I wanted to die alone.

My three girls were no better off during this period, as the divorce had been so very cruel and brutal. The oldest had been forced to stand up to her father and his cruel attacks, watching him try to destroy her mother before her eyes. In return, he had punished her by withholding money, his only commodity. The middle daughter had not spoken to me for several years, and the baby was missing in action as well—eaten up, I can only assume, with guilt and an abundance of immaturity. We were all drifting in our own worlds, trying to figure out where our family had gone and how to live again.

I had long ago begun starting each and every day with God. I wanted to give Him my first and best time. I began watching the numerous Christian channels for two to three hours, secretly begging to hear a word from God telling me it would get better. This time would prepare me for my prayer before I read my Bible. I prayed from the floor with my face on my Bible, weeping before the throne of grace. I would beg and plead for my children and for their pitiful lives to change, and that the younger two would remember that they loved their mommy, again. I had five years of this routine: praying, pleading, reading my Bible, exercising, and then leaving the house with no destination and not wanting to return.

I met Jack, and everything changed. A more tender and loving man does not exist. I was honest with him, spelling out my inadequacies and expecting him to run, not walk. He gently took my hand and my heart, and I began my crawl toward healing. He loved me when I was fearful of loving again, and he held me during my endless nightmares. I was so broken, so beaten down and unable to cry—with the exception of during my prayers. I could not find emotion. Jack loved me with abandon.

I realized that in my life so many who were supposed to love me, didn't love. My mom, my oldest brother that helped DV in the divorce, and my three husbands had never loved me. I also realized that I had never loved before in the way I love Jack. I told him that I loved him forever and after that. I wanted to grow old with him, to watch our five children blossom, and eventually to die with him. I wanted to love him as if I had never been hurt and to take care of his heart.

Having said all of that, at this writing, Jack and I are no more. I learned about myself after he left. I had to lose him to cherish what we had. When we met, I was running from everything, and now I wanted to run to him. I wanted a family. I wanted to help him raise his precious little girl, teaching her much of what I have learned in life. I had lost my homes, my money, my children, and now the love of my life.

This time it is different; it is another test of my faith in the goodness of God and his promises. Having gone through the horror of the divorce, I now have a different perspective. I have quietly given this latest trial to God, and I pray much of the day for another chance with Jack.

Love is the most powerful emotion known to man. When we love, we are most like God, for He is love. Now I am healed enough to have confidence in my choices. *Here is my heart, Lord. Take it and seal it with your love.*

Scripture tells me, you don't fight *for* victory; you fight *from* victory. You trust and you trust and then you trust some more. You can't change the past, but you can change the future. I trust Jack with my heart, but more importantly, I trust God with my heart.

***** *****

That was then, and then there is now.

Gentle reader, I now write to you six years after all of the above pages were written. I have a new publisher and a new opportunity to add and enhance my narrative as to better explain my situations.

Jack did not come back to me. The time he was in my life was for a reason. I learned from the experience with Jack that I wanted to love again. I later met David.

I know this to be true. There exist many levels of love. There is love without surrender, there is convenient love but my needs come first...and then there is a love that has no boundary. David entered my life and nothing was the same. Happiness dwells on my face and great love lives in my home. As of this day of writing, we have been married two years, three weeks, and five days. I have more than I ever dreamed possible.

As I reread my story, I find it just as emotional as when I lived it. At times, I had to stop the process of my editing as it still harbors anguish. My little story was written from a place of great damage.

I am no longer living as an abused person but as someone who has lived it and learned how to handle the horror called my past. I go longer periods of time not remembering it and when I do, I just simply put it away.

My precious daughters are in my life, loving their mommy. Prayers answered. Two of them live six minutes away, and we talk or see each other daily. Unfortunately, the baby who was used against me, has confessed to me, not a day goes by that she is not sorrowful for what had happened. We have had opportunities to speak of the past and try to process it. I have learned that there will never be an understanding of evil. It just is.

Since the first edition of my book was published, I have heard via my website from people all over the world. Unfortunately, what happened to me is not as unique as you might think.

# Lessons Learned in the Pit, You Take to the Palace

*He heals the brokenhearted and binds up their wounds.* —Psalms 147:3

When God says He will do something, then we must believe He will. When He says *all*, He means *all*. Scripture is not a suggestion. We must get to the place where we believe and trust.

In Mark 9:17–24, the father of a distressed child comes to Jesus and asks Him for healing. In verse 22, the father says, "If you can do anything, take pity on us and help." "If you can?" said Jesus. "Everything is possible for him who believes." Why is this concept so difficult? I am training myself to take my eyes off the issue and keep them on the God I serve. In II Corinthians 5:7 it says that we live by faith, not by sight.

Scripture tells us that we have trials and tribulations to build our faith. If life was always chugging along swimmingly, would we ever grow? Would we ever learn to lean on our Savior in dire times?

My life has been this journey of tribulations. For the longest time, Job was my best friend. Much is to be learned from knowing the story of Job. Job 1:1 says that there lived a man whose name was

Job. This man was blameless and upright; he feared God and shunned evil.

Keep this in mind when you feel that life is threading against you and nothing makes sense. Read Job 1:6–7. One day the angels came to present themselves before the Lord, and Satan also came with them. The Lord said to Satan, "Where have you come from?" Satan answered the Lord, "From roaming through the earth and going back and forth in it." Also read I Peter 5:8, which tells us to be self-controlled and alert. Your enemy, the devil, prowls around like a roaring lion looking for someone to devour.

Take courage from the above scriptures. First and foremost, you might have trials and difficulties that were not earned by you. Job was said to be blameless. Also, notice that Satan must get permission from God to come after you. In verse 8, Satan taunted God, saying that Job was only blameless due to the hedge of protection that God had placed around him. So God allowed Satan to tackle Job's faith. But in verse 12, the Lord said to Satan, "Very well, then, everything he has is in your hands, but on the man himself do not lay a finger."

This is very comforting to me. God must permit everything ugly in our lives before Satan can do anything. Now piece together all the scriptures of God's eternal love for us. If you recall, Job endured losing his home, all his children, and the servants. Eventually, his body was covered with sores. At the point where Job was looking for relief by putting dust on his sores, his three friends showed up to cheer him on. They commenced to accuse Job of bringing his heartache upon himself. Job's wife told him to curse God and die. Then God spoke to Job about His own sovereignty in the universe, and Job got it. In Job 42:7, Job prayed for his friends. Then, almost immediately, scripture pointed to God's blessings for Job. In Job 42:10–16, God restored and doubled Job's possessions.

This story is quite reassuring. Look beyond the anguish you are momentarily experiencing, and know that our God is faithful. He is loving. He rewards faith. Hebrews 11:6 says that without faith it is impossible to please God, because anyone who comes to Him must believe that He exists and that He rewards those who earnestly seek Him.

On so many occasions, I have found myself feeling like Elijah. In I Kings 17:1–6, God tells Elijah to leave and proceed eastward to hide in the Kerith Ravine east of Jordan. Verse 4 says, "You will drink from the brook, and I have ordered the ravens to feed you there." Notice that Elijah did not question why he should go there, what he would do there, or how long he must stay there. When he obeyed without question, God took care of him via the ravens.

We must look at life outside of the box. Why is it easy to believe that God made all things and that He is sovereign, but then we question the truth of verse 6 that tells us that ravens brought him bread and meat in the morning and bread and meat in the evening, and he drank from the brook? God can and does perform the impossible. I believe from these verses that whenever God asks something of us, He is more than able to supply us with what we need to accomplish it.

Now I am prepared to speak of the lessons we take from the pit to the palace. In Genesis chapters 37–41, the story begins with Joseph, age seventeen, and his dream. He tells of his dream, and his ten brothers become jealous. God has indeed given Joseph a glimpse of his future in that dream, but at age seventeen he is emotionally and spiritually ill equipped to rise and take his place from what was presented in the dream. God will use all the hardships that happen over the next eighteen years to mold Joseph into the man he needs to be.

Fast-forward to where Joseph is thrown into a pit by his brothers and left to die. He is then taken by a caravan of Ishmaelite to be sold into slavery in Egypt, taken to Potiphar's house, and wrongly accused of impropriety with Potiphar's wife. For this, he is thrown into jail, where he interprets the dreams of two prisoners, and then sits and waits for them to remember him and rescue him. Whew!

Through all this turmoil, pain, and anguish, it is clear that Joseph did not take his eyes off God. How easy it would have been for him to speak of how unfair life had been for the past eighteen years? One day, the chief cupbearer to Pharaoh remembered Joseph and his ability to interpret dreams, and he tells Pharaoh Joseph's story.

Pharaoh sends for Joseph from his place in prison to come and interpret his personal and unsettling dream. This is the day that Joseph goes from the pit to the palace; ultimately to reign as second in command to Pharaoh. Galatians 6:9 says, "Let us not become weary in doing good, for at the proper time we will reap a harvest if we do not give up." This is a promise from God, not a suggestion. Hold onto this in your pit, and you will surely take your lessons into the palace where they will serve you well. Also, remember that when God restored Joseph, he awoke that day in prison, but by afternoon Joseph was second in command to Pharaoh.

Another comforting story in scripture tells of the time when Jesus came walking on the water during a storm. The disciples were gripped with fear over the storm and the rough waters. John 6:21 says, "Then they were willing to take him [Jesus] into the boat, and immediately the boat reached the other side." I take from this that when Jesus calms the storms in our lives, we can *immediately* be on the other side of the problem.

# Forgiveness: Never Easy, but Always Necessary

*For if you forgive others for their transgressions, your heavenly Father will also forgive you.* —Matthew 6:14

In the month just prior to the beginning of the end (my divorce), I began a forty-day prayer. It began with my putting my needs on a piece of paper and then forgetting about them. I then wrote down others' needs, which would be the basis for my forty days of praying for forty minutes each day. I was on day thirty-nine when my life exploded.

I repeated this process again after the divorce, praying forty days for forty minutes each day for the six people who had been purchased by DV to use against me. Words fail me to express just how difficult this was. I would mentally picture each one and pray an individual prayer. It does help the soul to pray for enemies, and it is hard to carry pent-up anger for someone while praying for them, even if they have carelessly wronged you for their own benefit.

I had let go of most of the negative feelings attached to each person by the end of the forty days—with the exception of DV. I allowed my extreme hurt and betrayal to eat at me, to consume me with the unfairness of what I had experienced. It took several more years before I released my anger against DV. It was so freeing. As it was with my abusive mom, DV is so very sad, and he cannot be a happy man. Life can seem very unfair, but scripture is full of an overabundance of reassurance that God's children do not suffer needlessly. Additionally, in the end God always takes care of those who come against you. You reap what you sow: greater than you sow, later than you sow, but you always reap it. It is a spiritual law.

# You Cannot Have a Testimony without a Test

*But the Lord has been my stronghold, and my God the rock of my*
*refuge.* —Psalms 95:22

*And the God of all grace who called you to his eternal glory in*
*Christ, after you have suffered a little while, will HIMSELF restore*
*you and make you strong, firm and steadfast. Amen.*
—I Peter 5:10

He is faithful to rescue.

# Bound for Hardbound: A Louisiana *Lagniappe*

Snippets from "Life According to Samantha":

I feel it prudent to show a lighter side to me and my outlook on life. May you smile or preferably laugh out loud.

Go big or go home!

** ** **

"Less is more." *Wrong!* Less is less, and more is more.

** ** **

I firmly believe that I can do anything…for five minutes.

** ** **

Upon hearing *anyone* saying humorous or witty comments, the answer always is, "I hate it when you are funnier than me!"

** ** **

A friend or a stranger can comment on travel, and this brings out of my mouth into the stratosphere, "I want to go, I want some, and it is my birthday!" In fact, every day is my birthday, as it is a game to see how many birthday cakes I can glean in a year. *I never celebrate my real birthday!*

** ** **

If you hear thunder and rain, quickly go to your porch and watch. It is God's awesome power on display for our private delight.

** ** **

Never forget to dance. I dance when I am happy, but more importantly, I dance when I am sad. It does the heart good to feel this way, losing yourself in music. In my hometown of Nowhere, most Saturday mornings begin with dancing at Fred's to a Cajun band singing *en Français* as it has been since time began, or least since I was a little girl. The music is broadcast on the radio, and all advertisements are in French.

** ** **

Having grown up in Louisiana, where our worst cooks are amazing, I have the belief that all food is good for you. You must remember we are a state that eats "parts" in a sauce of course. I see people giving up eating the joys of life as a way to stay fit or young, or for whatever reason one can rationalize. But you don't live longer: your life has become so boring that it just appears to be so.

** ** **

Upon seeing a rainbow, rejoice. It is God's promise never to destroy the Earth again by water. You will never have to build an ark. What a relief!

** ** **

When I look into my children's faces, it truly is the most beautiful sight to behold. I can never thank God enough for giving me my three babies.

** ** **

I truly believe that if one of anything is good, then three has got to be better.

** ** **

Ignorance is fixable, but stupidity is terminal. For far too long, I was ignorant.

** ** **

Try to laugh twice as much as you cry. As an abused child, I learned to do this as a survival tactic, and it has served me well.

** ** **

I love to cook and often have impromptu dinner parties. My guests are treated to various strange foods complete with beaucoup of desserts. To be invited back, every guest must tell me how wonderful the food is five times. This is your insurance of being invited back.

** ** **

Why buy a dog and bark yourself? I thank you, Australia, for being so clever.

** ** **

Life is not a dress rehearsal. Grab it with both hands and eat it with a spoon.

** ** **

All things are possible with God. Awaken every day expecting a miracle.

** ** **

One of my babies, being fair of skin, had freckles. When she would complain about the spots on her beautiful face, I would tell her that the spots were angel kisses. This appeased her.

** ** **

If you do not exercise every day, then you do not deserve to sleep! It is never a question if you will brush your teeth each day, so look at exercise in the same way.

** ** **

Patience is not only a virtue but a necessity as well. Take time to enjoy.

** ** **

One of my babies grew to be taller than her peers. This bothered her. I told her that she was perfect but to be kind, as the rest of the world was too short.

** ** **

Movies are best viewed under the influence of Milk Duds, buttered popcorn, and chocolate malt. The Milk Dud goes into the mouth first and is allowed to melt before being chewed. Then popcorn with malt is savored together.

** ** **

If men could only learn this lesson—much mileage is to be gained by compliments. In my world, being factual is not necessary—just say it.

** ** **

Teach yourself to listen to the still, small voice, as it is not intuition but God speaking to you.

** ** **

My last baby was born and placed on my tummy to view. She was less than one-minute old, and I told her the angels kissed her and sent her to me. Her name, from that moment on, has been Angel Baby.

** ** **

If your loved one snores while sleeping, change the way you think about it. Instead of being upset, remind yourself that this is the sound of love and that he or she is with you.

** ** **

Anyone who reads can develop head knowledge, which is inferior to heart knowledge.

** ** **

Dare to believe the impossible.

** ** **

Most days, I will send a text message to my girls with the same ongoing message: do not forget to be grateful today.

Many years ago, a red bird would fly into the glass window near my desk. He would hit his head over and over for hours. It disturbed me so much that I began to pray for this sad bird, as I knew it must hurt. I then began to notice that the bird would be in another part of the house, flying into the window as I watched. Over time, due to the bird's perseverance, he got my attention. This was prior to the destruction of my world called divorce and during a very sad time in my life.

Then one day, when I was sitting outside for breakfast in a remote place, a red bird alighted on my table! He crossed the ocean for me? After this, I imagined it was God sending me a message that He was with me. This turned into seeing red birds on a regular basis. I thought to myself, when I see three red birds in a row, I will know it is over…*my test.* Years later, *I saw three red birds in a row flying outside my window.*

# Epilogue

*Remember the word which Moses the servant of the Lord commanded you, saying, "The Lord your God gives you rest and will give you this land."* —Joshua 1:13

*And the weary are at rest.* —Job 3:17b

*Rest in the Lord and wait patiently for Him.* —Psalms 37:7a

*Wisdom rests in the heart of one who has understanding.* —Proverbs 14:33a

*And his resting place will be glorious.* —Isaiah 11:10c

*Do not destroy his resting place.* —Proverbs 25:15b

I have learned reams of knowledge, wisdom, and patience since I first began this journey of writing about my life. The emotional healing cannot be quantified.

To tell my story, I had to acknowledge that my trek contained a plethora of enlightenment, hatred, love, abuse, forgiveness, betrayal, greed, and fear. The day I finished the manuscript, I went for a long walk to process my thoughts. As I walked, I began a murmur into my heart, saying, "I am free!" The murmur transcended into a low voice. Before I returned home, I had to shout for all to hear, "I am free, I am free!"

The next morning was quite different. I awoke to the thought of, *what do I do now?* The manuscript lived in my laptop for several weeks, as I had not the courage to present my work. After all, I am just a skinny girl from Nowhere, Louisiana. Who would want to hear my heart, or my story? Having lived all the negative and destructive emotions with a scant few good ones thrown in, I decided that I could do this. Remember my belief that I can do anything for five minutes? I decided that I could present my soul to the world. I soon entered into a whirlwind of publishers, and so on. This became a book so fast that it made my head spin. I definitely took notice that this just might be a "God thing."

My manuscript is soon to be a book. I write my epilogue five months after I finished the manuscript, having written "The End" and "Amen." On occasion, I talk to friends about the title of being an author, but it feels like it belongs to someone else. This period of five months has brought me to reflection mode. I have come to realize that there are four complete stages in recovery. They appear in the order you receive them:

1.  Faith

2.  Trust

3.  Surrender

4. Rest

When we encounter a trial and a test of our identity in Christ, we begin with faith. Something dreadful happens, so we recount what we know of our knowledge of who God is and what scripture says about life on Earth. This stage usually is quite long, especially if the trial exacts a price of pain and anguish. Some people never leave this stage and more than likely do not win in the end. Remember that when God wants to take you to another level of belief in His goodness and promises, His patience in getting you there will far outlast yours. Faith comes from hearing and hearing by the word of Christ (Romans 11:17).

Trust will come as you delve into scriptures, extracting those verses that speak to your mountain. This process more than likely drives you to seek and glean places and people in the Bible who displayed great trust in God. You learn of Job and his painful trying experiences and on occasion are grateful that Job was Old Testament. Possibly you seek more relief and discover Joseph. Joseph, after eighteen years of unfair and underserved grief, wins. Good to know! The night terror now becomes "eighteen years!" Will I possibly be able to withstand such a trial?

You begin to talk about it with your understanding God-minded friends or Bible study mates. At this level in the trial, trust can and does waiver. You convince yourself one day that you can do this, only to awake in the night gripped in fear and trepidation. You may have head and heart knowledge, but trust can be as elusive as a butterfly in the wind. Great trust and then not-so-great trust as if a yo-yo comes and goes in a skilled hand. It is also possible to live in this stage, as it is incomplete to receive the "I am taking you to another level" reward.

Surrender is a sweet place to be, where you believe the test and trial has end in sight. Scripturally, *surrender* means *yield*. You are worn down and weary, so yielding can be confused with giving up. It is not so. Surrender means to yield to the plan of God. Your days are like, "OK, God, do what you have to do."

In the surrender stage, I would awake each day and remind myself that the day I was going to have was the day God had ordained or allowed. Many a day, I would end up not liking the day I had, with a mumble, grumble, and endless prayer request to just give the test a rest. I reached this stage three months ago. The faith and trust stage was my identity for an undeterminable amount of years.

Oh, for rest…the sweetest of all places to be. You must long for it. God longs for it for you. Resting in God's will is brand-new to this skinny girl. I arrived a few weeks ago, and it is quite sweet. To achieve rest, there is a conscious decision to stay in this place. Hopefully, all the lessons learned in the first three stages will easily allow this. I must say that it is born out of weary, but weary must contain an abundance of trust, faith, and surrender. Everyone gets weary, and it is not necessarily a sign of lack in an area.

"Let us not lose heart in doing good, for in due time we will reap if we do not grow weary" (Galatians 6:9). Resting looks and feels like surrender but has no concern for the day. It is what it is. God says, "I know the plans I have for you, to prosper you." How can we possible argue with this?

A day of rest awakens to hope that this might be the day the trial or test ends. If it does not end, you go to bed with the thought that tomorrow might bring the answers and the puzzle pieces to your doorway. You also maintain at the end of the day, when the answer has not arrived, that you are most certainly one day closer to relief. You know that, you know that you know God will not and cannot deny his promises for you.

# Give Me Back My Babies

On the day the divorce was finally over with, signed, sealed, and delivered, my oldest baby said, "You will get a happy mommy house. I know we will make it." The statement came after a sigh of relief that I would not have to look over my shoulder in trepidation anymore. No longer would my car be followed every time I left the driveway, and the fear of being put in jail for breaking into my own home's safe had come to an end. The happy mommy house statement has stayed with me over the years. I wondered what this would look like and how I could possibly start over. On this first day of freedom, my oldest was with me cheering me on.

I will never forget her constant concern for her mommy. When the baby, baby was suddenly no longer with me in the beginning of the annihilation, the oldest would "beg me to live." I had never been without my babies and her concern was so great, forged out of my extreme loss of weight and insomnia. She was unwavering in her belief that all was wrong within her family upheaval. Without a doubt, her stance came from great loyalty due to her maturity and age. She was in an emotional place to see what was happening and possessed a maturity that the other two did not have due to their tender years and conditioning by their father.

She has since obtained her second master's degree from a prestigious university, obtaining it in only one year. She is quite successful and well thought of in her field. My precious middle baby has come back to her mommy. We spent the better part of five years apart. I never had any negative thoughts for her, other than knowing that she was being manipulated by her father to think untruths about her mommy.

For so many years, I would pray early in the morning and then throughout the day. I would shout, "Give me back my babies!" I never doubted that this would eventually take place, as all four of us were very close before they were used in the scheme. I just did not want to go through the valley without them.

Middle baby came back slowly, and we began the process of getting to know each other. She had matured into a young lady with immense talents. I had been forever changed by our circumstances. We realized that we loved each other but that we also liked each other as well. She is my buddy, my confidant, and my friend. I am her confidant as well. I told her that when you lose something and then get it back, it becomes more precious than before it was lost.

My middle baby has so many areas of great talent, and she is a success in life. She has several businesses in the arts, and has been published. One day you will read about her; you just will not know who she is.

My baby, baby, and I are in the process of healing. We did spend many years amid the in-and-out stages of various forms of forgiveness. We have lost so much due to the greed that put us in this place. She lost the ability to lean on her mommy in her early teenage years, and I lost the right to teach her the important values that I hold dear to my heart.

During the period of separation and divorce, this had to be a scary and terribly uncertain circumstance for my baby, baby. We had little communication, as DV did his best to keep us apart. Many a time he would schedule events for her on the night I could see her. I would take her to the tutoring or wherever only to sit in the car, and then my time would almost be up and she would return to him. My "Mini Me" and I grew apart. She was so young, vulnerable, and naive. She was no match for DV's cunning schemes.

There was an incident when I went to school to take her to a function on my night to be with her, only to be asked by the principal's office to stand outside. I had to leave the building! My embarrassment had reached new highs. They had orders from DV that he had to be informed if I showed up. How can this be? Even drug addicts get to keep their children! His housekeeper could take her from school, but the woman who nurtured her and taught her to walk and talk and love God had to get permission!

We had many episodes over the years where we would attempt to get close and then drift apart again. My heart broke at each juncture of her not being present in my life. Last summer was a turning point for me. I was sitting in church listening to an amazing sermon. The topic was forgiveness. I listened and contemplated, and my heart quickened. I immediately went to my car and sent a text to my baby stating that I wanted her in my life. In my heart, I asked for amnesia.

I had longed for the day that the court records would be amended and my good name restored. I held on, wanting a reprieve in writing that I was indeed a great mom. This is not going to happen. The proof of this is in the love I have for my babies. It *cannot* waiver. They are my life. DV may have bought "his truth" for a period of time. God will correct all injustices.

I have learned in my travels down this dusty winding road that when we experience a horror, it never goes away. You live with it in the recesses of memory, and on occasion it emerges. You examine it and then you put it away. You are always aware of the memories, but putting them away becomes easier and easier.

I did find the happy mommy house, and each baby has a room. They have a home. We have a family. The family may look different, but we are a bonded-together family, growing each day and learning to trust again.

And as is written upon each life raft: you are not a survivor until you have been rescued.

# My Epiphany

The past few months have held many revelations. My thoughts, heart, and soul-searching emotions are now becoming a book. The manuscript that lived in my computer is in production with many bits to do and finish before it becomes shelf-worthy.

I say this as I write—it does not seem a reality. I think about the ramifications of inscribing raw and vulnerable emotions, and the outcome of people I don't know (or more importantly, the people I do know) peering inside of me. Having said this, when friends or new acquaintances inquire as to the status of my book, I have one answer. *"Please do not read my book!"* I am always met with surprise and skepticism at such a statement.

I have not informed anyone at this point that the way the book was written was, I received the title first and then the title inspired my writings. I would say to people that the title wrote it: *A Love Story: How God Pursued Me and Found Me: An Impossibly True Story.* When I would sit at my laptop to write, I would first pray for God to guide my hands and thoughts. After doing this, my hands would fly at the keyboard without a pause in sight. I wrote every day, and the manuscript was finished in less than two months. I find this astounding, as I had been convinced that I only had a maximum of thirty words in my head!

One evening when I was out with friends, a group discussion arose about my book. I said my usual "Please do not read my book!" On my ride home at the end of a great night of conversations, I tossed about in my head, *why do I consistently ask people not to read my book?* My drive back to the house was a bit long, so I maintained this question in my heart. I need to mention at this juncture that this was a Saturday night. I began to marinate in the thought of writing a manuscript, submitting it to be published, and not wanting anyone to read it. I am not this absurd...even on a good day.

Before I arrived at my destination, I came to the conclusion and called it an epiphany. My epiphany was, "I wrote the book to myself!" Wow! This was big, as I now had answers to why I allowed myself to be so vulnerable. I needed to hear myself affirm that, though my life had an abundance of grief, there indeed was a plan. My thoughts began to center on how cathartic writing was, and then my healing became immeasurable. It made sense that if I had put all the emotions on the table for *me* to see, then this must have been my healing route. Right?

The morning after my revelation, I was sitting in church smiling. My thoughts were back to the epiphany. I was quite happy to figure out the "whys" of not wanting anyone to read it. God must have been leading me to an understanding!

I experienced a jolting thought that did not come through my brain. I heard God so very clearly, and He said to me, "You did not write the book to yourself. I wrote it to you!" *A Love Story: How God Pursued Me and Found Me.* What a love story, as He took my fingers at the keyboard and filled my heart with so many memories, some not thought of in many a decade.

In writing this last statement, I recall the scripture that says that God is not in the wind, nor is He in the thunder, but He is in the still, small voice resonating in our hearts.